Britain's Most
Notorious Prisoners

TRUE CRIME FROM WHARNCLIFFE

Foul Deeds and Suspicious Deaths Series

Barking, Dagenham & Chadwell Heath
Barnsley
Bath
Bedford
Birmingham
More Foul Deeds Birmingham
Black Country
Blackburn and Hyndburn
Bolton
Bradford
Brighton
Bristol
Cambridge
Carlisle
Chesterfield
Cumbria
More Foul Deeds Chesterfield
Colchester
Coventry
Croydon
Derby
Durham
Ealing
Fens
Folkstone and Dover
Grimsby
Guernsey
Guildford
Halifax
Hampstead, Holborn and St Pancras
Huddersfield

Hull
Jersey
Leeds
Leicester
Lewisham and Deptford
Liverpool
London's East End
London's West End
Manchester
Mansfield
More Foul Deeds Wakefield
Newcastle
Newport
Norfolk
Northampton
Nottingham
Oxfordshire
Pontefract and Castleford
Portsmouth
Rotherham
Scunthorpe
Sheffield
Southend-on-Sea
Southport
Staffordshire and the Potteries
Stratford and South Warwickshire
Tees
Warwickshire
Wigan
York

OTHER TRUE CRIME BOOKS FROM WHARNCLIFFE

A-Z of London Murders
A-Z of Yorkshire Murders
Black Barnsley
Brighton Crime and Vice 1800-2000
Durham Executions
Essex Murders
Executions & Hangings in Newcastle
and Morpeth
Norfolk Mayhem and Murder

Norwich Murders
Strangeways Hanged
Unsolved Murders in Victorian &
Edwardian London
Unsolved Norfolk Murders
Unsolved Yorkshire Murders
Warwickshire's Murderous Women
Yorkshire Hangmen
Yorkshire's Murderous Women

*Please contact us via any of the methods below for more information
or a catalogue*
WHARNCLIFFE BOOKS
47 Church Street, Barnsley, South Yorkshire, S70 2AS
Tel: 01226 734555 • 734222 • Fax: 01226 734438
email: enquiries@pen-and-sword.co.uk
website: www.wharncliffebooks.co.uk

BRITAIN'S MOST NOTORIOUS PRISONERS

Victorian to Present-Day Cases

STEPHEN WADE

First Published in Great Britain in 2011 by
Wharncliffe Books
an imprint of
Pen and Sword Books Ltd.
47 Church Street
Barnsley
South Yorkshire
S70 2AS

Copyright © Stephen Wade 2011

ISBN: 978-1-84563-129-1

Typeset in 11/13pt Plantin by Concept, Huddersfield.

Printed and bound in England by
the MPG Books Group.

Pen & Sword Books Ltd incorporates the Imprints of Pen
& Sword Aviation, Pen & Sword Maritime, Pen & Sword
Military, Wharncliffe Local History, Pen & Sword Select,
Pen & Sword Military Classics, Leo Cooper, Remember
When, Seaforth Publishing and Frontline Publishing.

For a complete list of Pen & Sword titles please contact
PEN & SWORD BOOKS LIMITED
47 Church Street
Barnsley
South Yorkshire
S70 2BR
England
E-mail: enquiries@pen-and-sword.co.uk
Website: www.pen-and-sword.co.uk

Contents

Introduction

The word 'notorious' implies a high level of very doubtful and often disturbing fame; it refers to the kind of fame that most of us would wish to avoid. Yet, in the world of true crime, it often has a reversal of those implications, and that is not merely because of the often wrongful assumption that readers of the genre go to it for the unhealthy frisson of blood and suffering in the tale. In fact, history shows that 'notorious' may imply all kinds of references, including the humorous and bizarre.

Notorious may be local, but also be so bizarre that the weirdness spreads across culture, as with the case of Allison Johnson, who stood in Lincoln Crown Court in 1992, charged with aggravated burglary. He was known across the prison establishment and beyond as 'the cutlery man' because he tended to swallow knives, forks and spoons. Johnson was a repeat prisoner but actually spent more time on the operating table than in a 'pad'. Peter Seddon, writing about the case, joked that as the man walked from court, he was 'severely rattled'.

There are humorous and strange tales in this book, but often only incidentally. In a prison community in Britain, there is an unusual kind of humour, parallel in some ways to the 'canteen culture' of those professions that deal with the less pleasant and normal side of life. It is hard but also somehow infantile, basic and sometimes witty and inventive. A notorious prisoner, in that context, can actually be an entertaining one, but that is something we have to understand in a way completely separate from his or her crimes. The truth is that a criminal's life, if a long jail stretch is involved, is an odd mix of surreal adventure and crushingly tedious routine.

Of course, the stories here will not all be of this kind in the range of meanings of the word 'notorious'. My tales include the prison lives of serial killers: terrifyingly deviant minds who need the fantasy in their sick imaginations to be lived out in a horrendous drama involving real and innocent victims. But, paradoxically to those who do not know a prison community, the two sit quite easily together: the crazy, entertaining and the horrible aspects can live together in that complex establishment, the prison.

Writing about prisoners invariably entails explaining prisons, so I begin with that explanation as a prelude to the stories. These stories also involve some crime history: I begin with some late Victorian cases simply because they are compelling stories, and then move into the more recent sensations of such guests of Her Majesty as Charles Bronson and Ian Brady. The Victorian and Edwardian stories necessarily bring together the shadow of the noose and the horrors of a prison system that was effectively compared to a miserable purgatory as sick and inhuman as anything in Dante's vision of that state of limbo. To be in a prison is to forget time, or at least to see it differently. But when the prisoner in question is Florence Maybrick, for example, waiting for the day when the hangman would call, it is a very different matter to that of the modern serial killer who, for whatever reasons, will rot in jail, but with regular meals, a well-stocked library at his disposal, and some of the wonders of the age of the machine.

The selection of stories here was difficult to make; the emphasis had to be on people living between c.1950 and today, with some earlier examples which were too interesting to resist. What added piquancy and not a small amount of vicarious pleasure was the fact that some of the subjects here have spent decades behind bars and, common sense will tell us, that changes people in radical ways. There are sometimes complete transformations.

In my years working as a writer in prisons, with both men and women prisoners, I met dozens of lifers, and some who were destined to be 'life meaning life' prisoners. In one case, I had the clearest transmutation of a personality I ever met with. This was a man who had committed a double murder and who had been inside for eighteen years when I met him. He had amazingly changed his life and thought; he was a Buddhist; he had learned to play a musical instrument, and he taught and led meditation sessions in the jail. His body was lithe and supple; he worked out with his mind, not always his body, and he gave gentle, direct advice to those who asked for it. He was the most quiet, restrained and self-controlled person you could ever meet. Yet, as some readers will be thinking, what would he be like outside? That question nags at you like a child tugging at its mother's coat.

How can we know for sure about that transformation? The tabloids are always eager to tell the public about the latest psychopath who has been released from prison, not considered to be a danger to the public, who promptly slits the nearest throat or who rapes the first woman he meets. Not only that, but the nature of expert testimony in the dock has been challenged and has become a flexible concept rather than a reliable forensic element in a trial. Only DNA has superseded the traditional 'boffin' who presents the arcane learning relevant to an extreme and repulsive crime.

In the end, the choice of subjects was dictated by their sheer inescapable notoriety: I do not mean that simply in the sense of their list of killings or robberies. The notoriety has been partly the result of the media interest of course. A person is made notorious by those who wish to disseminate interest and sensation around the personality. For that reason, there is an element of eccentricity sometimes as well as the shuddering personality we know from creations such as Hannibal Lector on the screen, or from the pages of the crime novelists who feel drawn to invent repulsive tales where there is no need to elaborate on the evil that is clearly there in the real narratives of crime.

In a book such as this, we also need to be sure about some basic concepts. Some of the people in these pages have done the most shocking and amoral acts the twisted imagination could invent. We therefore ask, is there such a thing as evil? I have no hesitation is saying yes. I offer a very confident affirmative here. I have met and worked with murderers of all kinds, from the men and women who kill from within the routine framework of their normal lives, and kill with intention – with what the law calls 'mens rea' and an 'actus reus' – that is they make a decision to take a life and they do so. But those occasions are often when a person is pushed to an extreme or suffer from a moment of irrational urge, something outside their personality profile. Then there are the others, and at times I have looked into their eyes. They have evil living in them like a birthmark stain on the skin. It is there, it is apparent, and it cannot be washed away.

I have worked with some killers who have no notion of remorse. One man painted and drew his crime scenes, but in disguise. He found a way to depict them by indirect means; others have spoken to me about how and why they took lives, and made it seem rational, as if anyone would have killed the person in question. There are also inexplicable elements here, such as the man who walked into my creative writing class, a broad smile on his face, and said, 'You're the right bloke aren't you? Well, here's what I've written ... it's about when I killed my wife!' The smile never left his face, and he walked out, leaving the two sheets of neatly-written words of murder for me to chew over.

The chapters therefore include some prisoners whose lives are generally well known, but also others whose prison lives are less familiar. The stress here is on their prison lives. For instance, there are libraries of books available on Peter Sutcliffe and his crimes, but not so much on his prison life. There are interesting sources too, some previously unknown. For example, I was once in a jail when I read a file of letters, and one of these, to the extent of four pages, was from Charles Bronson, to the Education manager, describing, clearly and powerfully, how much he had derived great satisfaction from working with a group of special needs people who had come into the prison to spend time in the gym with selected prisoners. Mr Bronson was lyrical in his expression of delight and satisfaction at being of some help to those guests of the jail.

There is also the question of the time spent behind bars. Some of the subjects here were waiting in jail only a few days or weeks, before they walked to the scaffold. But today, the issue of 'life meaning life' presents knotty legal and penal features in a life sentence. The basic pattern is that a life sentence is given and then the judge sets a minimum time of incarceration, or a definite time period. After that it is a matter of appeals and parole. A determinate sentence is such that the prisoner must be released after that set period of time or 'tariff'. An indeterminate sentence means that the person has been sentenced to life for public protection (IPP abbreviation is often used); an IPP prisoner will serve the minimum stated, and there will only be a release when the Parole Board is satisfied that the person is no longer a danger to the public.

Life sentences have to be given if the conviction is for murder, but life may be given for many other offences such as rape, manslaughter or arson. But some of the prisoners here are under a mandatory life sentence. This is the only sentence which can be given to an adult convicted of murder. There is also the sentence entailing 'during Her Majesty's Pleasure' and this can be given to anyone over ten years of age but under eighteen years when the offence was committed. Murderers between eighteen and twenty-one at the time of the offence may have a mandatory sentence of custody for life.

Before April 2005 there were 'automatic life sentences' – applying to people who were over eighteen on or after the 1 October 1997, and convicted of a second serious, violent or sexual offence. This was replaced by the notion of IPP in 2005, but some lifers in the system are still there under the automatic sentences.

Lifers and others with long sentences are also subject to the confusion which has arisen over the last ten years with regard to laws on sentencing. In a ruling at the Court of Appeal, Criminal Division, in December 2009, for instance, Lord Justices Hughes, Rafferty and Hedley removed a ridiculous unfairness: owing to the way in which sentencing legislation had been effected, there was a distinct anomaly: a defendant sentenced with two consecutive periods under two different regimes would not have the same eligibility for release on a tagging/curfew mode as early as a person with one single sentence of the same length. With these situations in mind the judges ruled that this be corrected and made just. Prisoners doing a long tariff are faced with these complexities, and in the prison newspaper, *Inside Time,* there is a regular and lengthy feature explaining sentencing legislation in layman's terms.

There are a small number of prisoners who have to be locked up under a whole life order. The Prison Service defines this with these words: 'Where the trial judge has decided that the requirements of retribution and deterrence can be satisfied only by prisoners remaining in prison for the rest of their lives, the trial judge will not set a minimum term of imprisonment . . .' In July 2009 there were 10,900 prisoners serving an indeterminate sentence and just over 300 of these were women.

In my own life 'inside' I was always gathering material for what I knew was to be a book about prisons in some way. I never thought it would be this one, but my experiences have naturally fed into it. My own incarceration was accidental: I was locked up for an hour, with an inmate who was also a keen writer, and I never noticed that the key had been turned. Trying to imagine what that must be like for forty years is beyond imagination, yet that happened to John Straffen, and he had no other fellow writer to talk to and pass the time.

Timeline of Prison History

1777   John Howard published *The State of the Prisons,* a survey and critique of all local gaols

1791   Jeremy Bentham proposes his idea for a penitentiary

1811   The Select Committee on Penitentiary Houses recommends a penitentiary be built at Millbank (the current site of Tate Modern)

1820   The flogging of women prisoners is abolished

1830s   The 'Silent System' introduced

1843   The Millbank experiment fails: the prison is closed

1856   The first recommendation that hanging is done in private, inside the walls

1863   The Carnarvon Committee recommends a regime more attuned to punishment

1863   Broadmoor opened as Broadmoor Criminal Lunatic Asylum

1867   The end of convict transportation

1868   Hanging is made private

1895   The Departmental Committee on Prisons indicates that there should be another switch, from a stress on punishment to an investment in rehabilitation

1898   The crank and the treadmill were finally abolished

1908   The Borstal Act establishes the first juvenile offenders scheme with the new ideas of a standardised regime in place. This was for people aged between sixteen and twenty-one

1917   Dartmoor receives over a thousand 'conscientious objectors'

1932   Mutiny at Dartmoor

1946   A serious mutiny at Northallerton prison

1948   Military drill introduced at detention centres

1976   Serious riot at HMP Hull

1983   Charles Bronson stages a rooftop protest at Broadmoor

1990   Riots in Dartmoor

1991   The Criminal Justice Act: 'integral sanitation' introduced. In other words, 'slopping out' ended

1995   Ronnie Kray dies

1999   Charles Bronson takes an education officer hostage at HMP Hull

2000   Reggie Kray is released from prison on compassionate grounds, and dies a few weeks afterwards

2007   'The Istanbul Statement' – puts forward the guideline that solitary confinement should be prohibited for death row prisoners and life-sentenced prisoners, for mentally ill prisoners and children under eighteen

CHAPTER 1

Inside Oblivion: Then and Now

The people figuring prominently in these chapters provide a miscellany of the criminals in the average prison population anywhere at any given time. That is, some are hardened villains and some are unfortunates who made the wrong decision at the wrong time and in the wrong place. Prison kills time so that it stays dead, and after the first shock it's all about survival. That sounds simpler than it really is. In fact, that survival depends on the ability to project, to perform, to have 'front'.

A man who had done almost twenty years inside told me that there were three versions of him, each one being a variety of himself. There is the man who walks out and becomes the survivor on the wings; there is the other one who is the person his family wants to see and hear when there is a visit or a phone call, and the third one is the man alone, in the cell, with just his thoughts and his own company. One man may hate the self he is alone with: everything he does inside is to escape that self; but another may genuinely want to use the time inside to find out the real self that has been hiding behind fists, hatred, drugs or drink.

What about the place itself? If we think of a Victorian local jail, then the place is a fortress: a huge central tower and radiating wings from the centre, all plain for supervision. Then there are four levels and the nets between to save the lives of the would-be suicides or the potential victims. These make the huge expanse of the prison wing look like a sprawling web, with metal walkways. In fact, everything is metal: the floors, cell doors, railings, bars: hard, dull and relentless metal, as if the place is some kind of factory. In a way it is. The Victorians came to believe that reformation and change, the crushing of the villain inside, began with silence and contemplation, followed by work and prayer. Renewal would lead to redemption in the right circumstances. The basis of that thinking was change, transmutation. Naively, they believed in rehabilitation as the end of a process. Today, change is rare and many prisoners want to stay behind bars: it is their chosen place of life, as they cannot cope anywhere else. Three square meals a day, literacy classes, television and evening recreation are on offer. There is no possibility of a stroll round to the local boozer, but at least no bills drop through the letter box.

That scenario may be right for the everyday criminals, but the gallery of villains or victims in the following pages are mostly (with the exception of Wilde, Ellis and de Valera) characters with psychopathic tendencies or seriously dangerous elements in their lifestyle. To be fair, some of the notorious prisoners here have reformed, so the theme is not that of the average 'thrill kill' true crime book. On the contrary, these profiles are about offences and personalities across a wide spectrum. For instance, Noel Razor Smith, writer and prisoner, has openly said that he wants his books to provide beneficial influences on other people who may follow his trajectory into crime.

This point introduces the idea of prison as a strangely quasi-religious place for some of its denizens. I have known several people who, in their time out within the walls of our penal colonies, have 'found religion' and not simply because talking with the chaplain means free tea and biscuits (though such motives are not unknown). There is, oddly, a monkish aspect to life in the pad and on the wing. After all, most versions of sensuality and instant gratification of the senses tend to be on hold when inside, and many of the profiles here involve prisoners who have had to take a cocktail of drugs, for the better working of the prison daily regime and the peace and order of all concerned.

The prison chapel is a very special place and always has been. In the case of de Valera, it was the source of his means of escape. But for many today and in the past, it has been the one area in the prison in which there is a feeling that a burden is temporarily lifted. It can be a hiding place in a spiritual sense; it may also be the only place where meditation and quiet are possible. In my prison work, it was where the drama group met, or where talks could be given. But generally, it has been special in all kinds of contexts.

But there is no way that a book like this may overlook or omit the really important aspect of prison life: the loss of freedom. People have expressed to me the view that the purpose of prison is to have a dark place where we can throw a criminal and then piss on him. The do-gooders such as myself, walking around the wings recruiting people for creative writing projects or acting, we run the risk of being, through the eyes of the professionals, 'care bears'. That phrase is used today inside for 'civilians' with good intentions, plans of providing opportunities for self-development and so on.

Some of the prisoners in this book have of course flowered and impressed as creative souls, and Charles Bronson is among them, but in the end, it is hard to keep away the glamour and charisma of the real criminal, the one who has given the right expletives to the 'screws' and the establishment of law. One man, a London gang member, once said to me, 'I shouldn't be in here ... I'm in here because of their law ... my law is different, see. I don't live by their law, and never did, mate.' He was expressive and ebullient when it came to opinions on the criminal justice system, with his favourite phrase, 'Fuck the laws of England, it's made by toffs' usually on his lips. The man was beyond redemption because in his head he lived in a nation free from legal restraint. His credo was 'I could, so I did.'

The prisoners here, then, are mostly inhabitants of a prison community for the regular reasons of having done something extreme and repulsive to those who have a moral universe around them which they recognise and obey. But there are also those who are 'political' – the spies and the gun-runner and the statesman. This has always been an issue inside. Back in the 1830s, when Chartists were thrown into houses of correction up and down the land, they usually insisted that they would not do their time on the repulsive treadmill because they were 'political' prisoners, not thugs, killers or robbers. They were there because they had dared to believe in something that the current government did not want to create or encourage.

That division is hard to apply to someone such as William Joyce, of course, the man who broadcast Nazi propaganda in

World War Two. Equally, the German spies who ended their lives dancing on a gallows rope were, after all, fighting for their country. With these kinds of contrasts in mind, the reader will have to make up his or her mind about the moral or philosophical dimensions on criminal biographies. Surely one of the key insights and areas of fascination about a criminal act is how it relates to a moral structure: morality and law are awkward but inseparable twins, difficult to manage and explain.

Yet, it has to be admitted that some prisoners are notorious because their transgression has been something so extreme that it is inexplicable. Evil, yes, however that word is defined and whatever it is conceived to be as part of something done by a human being. There are serial killers among the notorious, and despite all the advances in medical and psychological knowledge, there is still no consensus on what the common ground is in psychopathy in that respect. We are still left with the images in popular culture of serial killers as beasts, monsters, amoral fetishists of death. Of course, that interpretation, as a media 'spin' is easy to achieve, but something lies deeper, and it may be explained by research, as work by Blair has shown, as he attempts to find a physiological basis for psychopathy. His book, *The Psychopath: Emotion and the Brain*, provides some kind of basis for believing that explanations may soon be established. Meanwhile, the programmes go on being made, and the headlines still appear regularly, concerning serial killers or term-of-life prisoners being subjected to attacks while in jail. The public is made to relish the latest gory image of the serial killer or child killer, seen after a vicious attack.

With all these considerations in mind, it is hoped that the reasons for my selection of notorious prisoners have been made clear. The final element of prison life which has to be made explicit is that it has stunning extremes of behaviour within the Establishment. I have known cases in which young men have managed to take their own lives using only a tap and some string; there are self-harmers behind bars who have so many wounds and cuts along all limbs that they move to the skin by the groin; there are so-called vulnerable prisoners who live in fear, like rats in the dark, and there are many, many mentally ill people in our prisons.

These stories may be considered to be 'highlights' from the present and from recent history, presenting when assembled a kaleidoscope of notoriety, ranging from the repulsive to the strangely entertaining.

CHAPTER 2

Florence Maybrick: Ready for the Noose

From her cell in Woking Invalid Convict prison, Florence Maybrick saw and carefully noted the best and the worst of the British penal system as it was at the end of the Victorian period. She had been moved there from Aylesbury prison, where she had been brought out of solitary confinement to be told that she was bound for a convict prison. In some ways that was a better place to be than a county prison, but for Florence, who had been used to a comfortable suburban middle class life in Liverpool, and before that in America, this was disgusting and degrading. As we say today, with a tinge of cruel irony, welcome to jail, Madame. But first we have to explain how she came to be behind bars in 1889.

In the nineteenth century, the ubiquity of fly-papers in the average home was something that could lead from routine habits to a suggestion of heinous foul play. They were a neat way to rid the house of insects, but when they were soaked, for arsenic to be extracted for other uses, there could be trouble. In Battlecrease House, in Aigburth, this was a factor in the puzzling and desperately sad story of Florence Maybrick. To make matters worse for her, she was married to man who enjoyed taking tiny quantities of poison, for all kinds of reasons.

When that man, James Maybrick, died, the finger of guilt pointed at his wife. The story went on to become not only a famous and controversial case, but a story that has been acquired by the vast library of Jack the Ripper theories, as James was in the habit of visiting London, and his strange personality gave rise to a certain line of enquiry about him.

The story of the Maybricks began when James was on board the liner *Baltic* in 1880. There he met young Florence, only eighteen at the time, and Maybrick was forty-two. Florence had been born in Mobile, Alabama; her mother aspired to wealth and status and wanted the same for her daughter. Mrs Maybrick's third husband had been a German aristocrat, and so the American lady was actually no less than the Baroness von Roques if she wanted to pull rank or put on airs. James Maybrick, along with many other men, found Florence to be very alluring. She was an attractive blonde, blue-eyed and very shapely. It must have been a stunning contrast for her when they married and moved to Liverpool, after living first in Norfolk, Virginia, for a while.

After they married in 1881, they settled at Battlecrease House in Aigburth; the place is a huge building, and Maybrick had acquired considerable wealth in the cotton business. But the change in lifestyle and cultural ambience must have been depressing for the young bride. She was a product of the American South, and of the wealthy, socialising element of that culture. Now she was in a British suburb of a fast-growing industrial city with a very sombre and grey climate. Society and social gatherings were limited for her, and her husband was often away from home.

They had children, and on the surface at least they would have appeared to be like every other middle-class couple. But the main problem lay with James. As time went on, his business floundered. Not only was he failing in commerce, but in his personality he was nurturing habits that would ruin his health. Maybrick was drawn to the questionable pleasures of taking poisons and drugs to keep an edge on life (in fact to enhance sexual potency, as arsenic was taken to do). He also lived the fairly typical double life of the Victorian married man: attentive husband at home but malcontented womaniser when he could find the time and opportunity.

Clearly, Florence would soon find the stress of this relationship, and the loneliness it imposed on her, too much to handle. The fact that Maybrick then set about saving money at home by imposing privations and discipline on the domestic routine was perhaps the last straw. She wrote to her mother (living in Paris at the time) that she was in a mood to leave the house and move elsewhere, and doubted that 'life was worth living', things were so bad. Her situation was ripe for the relief, pleasure and

fulfilment that an affair would bring. She found the man in
Alfred Brierley, a man in the same line of business as James.

Her mistake, as we look on her life with the knowledge of
hindsight, was that she was not discrete. She and Brierley would
have times together in London posing as a married couple. But
her strains at the hands of Maybrick were intolerable. He had a
mistress, and she equally became rash about her attempts to find
pleasure outside marriage. There was an element of torment
in their relationship, even to the point of Florence flirting with
James's brother, Edwin. Things were moving towards some
kind of crisis; they were not sleeping together, and Florence was
thinking about leaving him.

At this point, enter the fly-papers. Because she was in the
habit of using a mixture of arsenic and elderflower to treat boils
on her face, the soaking papers were a common sight in the
house. But then came James's illness. On 27 April, he was ill and
he blamed this on a prescription of strychnine being wrongly
calculated. This would have made sense of a man with those
strange habits of pleasure. But his health began to decline more
severely. Fate was stacking the odds against Florence, as the
servants were noticing the soaking fly-papers and linking that
to their master's decline. After all, he had cut her from his will
and had been insulting and aggressive towards her on many
occasions. She had cause to detest him. The illness dragged on,
and a nurse was employed to be with the patient at all times.

Maybrick's brother, Edwin, also came, and he took charge of
things. The situation then was that Florence was estranged from
her man; she was seen as potentially a deranged woman with a
grudge against her husband, and there was evidence mounting
against her with regard to the arsenic. Even worse, bearing in
mind the morality of the time, she wrote to her lover, Brierley,
trying to arrange a meeting with him before he left the country;
in that letter she referred to Maybrick's condition and noted that
he had no suspicion of the affair. Florence was often present at
the sick man's bedside and unfortunately for her, she played a
part in using the medicines, saying that James had actually
asked her to give him some arsenic in powder form. Everything
she seemed to do in the role of nurse or caring wife turned into
facts to be used against her when Maybrick died, as he did

on 11 May. She was arrested on suspicion of wilful murder, by Superintendent Bryning.

The high drama continued even to the point of her mother entering the scene, there was a confrontation, and Florence put the situation very neatly, saying to her, 'They think I poisoned Jim.' She was taken first to Lark Lane station, and then to Walton gaol.

The trial began at St George's Hall on 31 July, and Sir Charles Russell led her defence. There was great confusion in the forensic and medical evidence, even to the point of two experts disagreeing about whether or not the deceased had died from arsenical poisoning. Events went against her, and in the end it could be said that Florence was a victim of the judge. This is because there was just so much testimony about Maybrick's habits of pumping his body full of drugs and poisons that he was dicing with death, anyway, and ruining his health for many years before these suspicions were first aroused about his wife's alleged designs on him. The judge, Mr Justice Fitzjames Stephen, directed his long summing-up to the likely guilt of Florence if certain facts were ignored: that is, he reinforced the accusations of moral lapses against her, to the detriment of the actual issue of murder. He was ludicrously biased in his dramatic account of the situation of slow poison on a supposed 'loved one'. Naturally, the jury would begin to turn against Florence and forget the contradictions about the actual nature and administering of the poison. Arguably, the judge's action which had the most impact on the jury was his mention of the letter to Brierley about Maybrick being 'sick unto death' and his very evident repugnance at what he was implying she had done and written with such callousness. The jury surely must have been influenced by seeing this. There was definitely 'reasonable doubt' in the case, and a death sentence was outrageous. Yet, on 7 August, Florence Maybrick was sentenced to hang. The judge, leaving the court, was the target of general public abuse and displeasure, so wrong was his sentence perceived to be.

The real heart of this sensational trial was Florence's loud assertion that she was innocent of this crime: 'I was guilty of intimacy with Mr Brierley, but I am not guilty of this crime.'

But the real sensation was yet to come; after the death sentence was passed on her. There was a strong and widespread campaign for clemency, and this was going on even at the time that Florence was waiting her fate in Walton prison (with gallows being made ready outside). The Home Secretary arranged a reprieve: the sentence was to be commuted to penal servitude for life. But in 1904 she was released and returned to America. There, as Richard Whittington-Egan has written, she hid herself away in the Berkshire foothills; she became 'Florence Chandler' in South Kent, Connecticut. The person who became the epitome of the dotty and lonely old spinster, surrounded by cats, as Whittington-Egan says, 'was known to successive generations of South Kent boys as *The Cat Woman*'. She died in 1941, aged eighty-one. History tells of two Florence Maybricks, then, but there is another – the lonely prisoner, unjustly incarcerated, in those silent years before release.

History has leaned to the view that gastroenteritis, not murder, led to Maybrick'sdeath.

In prison, Florence registered everything and she produced a book, *My Fifteen Lost Years*, after her release in 1904. This work gives us a tremendous amount of documentary information on life behind bars for women at that time. She expresses her condition in jail like this: 'Here I may state in general that I early found that thoughts of without and thoughts of within – those that haunted me of the world and those that were ever present in my surroundings – would not march together . . . the conflict between the two soon became unbearable . . .'

She reflected that her 'safety' was in 'compressing her thoughts to the smallest compass of mental existence'. Florence is accurate and powerful in her account of the visiting time – something that is as stressful today as ever it was. Her mother used to travel from France to see her, and the conditions they had at 'visits' are described in Florence's book: 'Whenever my mother's visit was announced, accompanied by a matron I passed into a small oblong room. There a grilled screen confronted me; a yard or two beyond was a second barrier . . . and behind it I could see my mother . . .'

She was the victim of something inherent in the prison system too – duped by another prisoner, using her for selfish means. The other prisoner gave her some fine wool for her stocking, after spilling hot water on her foot, and later there was a cell search (a 'spin') and the wool was found in her cell. She suffered greatly after that, as she wrote: 'I was degraded for a month to a lower stage, with a loss of twenty-six marks, and had six days added to my original sentence.'

But in January 1904 she was released. Florence had always said that she bought the arsenic for use on flypapers, ultimately to be used as a beauty treatment. After her death among her few possessions found was a piece of paper on which was written the method of adapting fly papers to cosmetic uses.

CHAPTER 3

The Ballad of Oscar Wilde

Oscar Wilde is arguably the most notorious literary prisoner in English literature, closely followed by John Bunyan. In his writing he had a lot to say about the prison regime in Britain at the end of the nineteenth century, and in his *Ballad of Reading Gaol*, he produced a classic of prison poetry.

In his essay, *De Profundis*, he wrote: 'While I was in Wandsworth prison I longed to die. It was my one desire. When after two months in the infirmary I was transferred here [to Reading] and found myself growing gradually better in physical health, I was filled with rage. I determined to commit suicide on the very day on which I left prison. After a time that evil mood passed away ...' We know now, thanks to the researches of Anthony Stokes, who is a senior prison officer at HMP Reading today, why conditions improved for Wilde in Reading. But he had had a terrible time.

Wilde's fall and disgrace are well known. His homosexual relationship with Lord Alfred Douglas, the son of the Marquis of Queensberry, led to a bitter confrontation with the Marquis, and eventually Wilde was in court, first after he took out proceedings against the Marquis for criminal libel (*libel* today) and then, after losing that action, he himself was charged with sodomy. He was found guilty and was sentenced to two years in prison; that was on 25 May 1895. First, he spent the weekend in Newgate, and was then taken by cab to Pentonville. So began his degradation. By the time he was moved to Reading gaol, he had experienced the worst of the prison system as it was at that time. Entry meant a strip search, followed by a medical examination and a bath; then he would have put on the prison clothes, with the black arrows, signifying that he was now no more than a chattel belonging to Her Majesty's government.

From the beginning, Wilde had problems with the food, and he was ill, suffering from diarrhoea. He could never really sleep properly; he was a large man and the bed was no more than a board, with one blanket. It was difficult to be warm at any time. But he was, in some sense, a celebrity prisoner and he had friends who had power: one such was no less than RB Haldane, who was a Prison Commissioner. Haldane took an interest in Wilde's case from the start. In June 1895, he visited Wilde and promised that he should have books, pen and ink. Such a thing was forbidden, but as events were to prove, there were many aspects of Wilde's prison life that involved breaking the rules.

There was a furore on the part of the Governor, but as is still the case today, there are exceptional circumstances in prison, and matters vary according to who the person is and what his condition may be. In Wilde's case, part of the reason for him having special treatment was that he was seriously ill. Deaths in prison are always embarrassing for the staff as well as for the prison service and the Home Secretary. With Haldane's help, Wilde read his books – fifteen altogether. Later he was to work in the prison library, and that was one of the most humane moves made on the part of the authorities.

Wilde was moved to Wandsworth in August 1895, and there his condition deteriorated even more: as already noted, there he wanted to die. Concern was expressed for his mental health, and a doctor was sent to look at him, along with some specialists from Broadmoor. It was decided that he was not mentally ill, but the Wandsworth period did nothing but harm to the public image of the man whose plays had once entertained the glitterati of London. A chaplain wrote to the newspapers to report on the fact that, while having an interview with Wilde, he had smelled semen. In the late 1890s, the time when the intellectuals were full of talk about the 'degeneration' of the human race, it was one of the worst things to happen to the man who was already, in the public opinion, the epitome of everything that was repulsive to the heterosexual, empire-building commuter class, with its mediocre and philistinistic views on high art as well as on moral stricture.

But Wilde was soon transferred to Reading, and there, as Anthony Stokes has discovered in his book, *Pit of Shame*, Wilde had friends who made his time inside much easier. But in

Reading there was an execution during Wilde's time there: a soldier called Wooldridge, of the Royal Horse Guards, had murdered his wife. Wilde's experience of seeing the man, and in fact, of even seeing the burial after the hanging, within the prison grounds, gave us the classic poem, *The Ballad of Reading Gaol*, in which we have the lines:

> *I walked with other souls in pain,*
> *Within another ring,*
> *And was wondering if the man had done*
> *A great or little thing,*
> *When a voice behind me whispered low,*
> *'That fellow's got to swing.'*

This reminds us that the spell in Reading was far from being paradise, but what he did have was a man on the panel of prison visitors who was instrumental in alleviating some of the pain of prison life for the great writer. We now know from Stokes' research that George W Palmer, of Huntley and Palmer, the biscuit manufacturer, was one of the prison visitors. At that time they were known as the Board of Visitors, whereas today they are the Independent Monitoring Board, and their role is to tour their allotted prison and enquire on conditions by speaking to prisoners in the daily routine. The Palmers' biscuit factory was next door to Reading gaol, and so Haldane's aim of looking after Oscar Wilde took another course, as well as being a source of books and paper.

There was another link between the Palmers and Wilde: just a few years before the trial, Wilde had been a visitor at the home of Palmer's younger brother, Walter, whose wife was a lady who liked to run a literary salon of a kind: Wilde had been to the biscuit factory in 1892, and signed the visitors' book. But there was also another measure taken to make Wilde's time at Reading more palatable; the first Governor had been a strict disciplinarian, and had no time for rules being bent or broken, so he was promoted to another prison, and the new Governor, Major Nelson, was far more sympathetic to Wilde's condition. That move was followed by the appointment of a warder called Martin, and he would become something of a special friend –

again, something that would not normally be tolerated in a prison establishment.

Yet, life was tough in Reading, of course. One of the saddest events there was when Wilde had lost the custody of his children and his wife, Constance, came to the prison. She saw him there for the very last time, as she died just a short time later. One biographer described the situation: 'Mrs Wilde cast one long lingering glance inside and saw the convict-poet, who in deep mental distress ... witnessed his degradation.'

Thomas Martin, in Stokes' view a 'plant' put there by Haldane to give Wilde special treatment, was indeed guilty of breaking all the rules concerning prison officers and prisoners. He took Wilde drinks and biscuits every day – something that is technically a criminal offence called trafficking. On the exterior of every prison wall in Britain, next to the front gate, is a notice defining trafficking and giving the public dire warning of the consequences of giving prisoners anything without clearance. Martin later wrote an account of his life with Wilde in Reading. Wilde's fall from grace and respect is nowhere better illustrated than in Martin's memory of him having to turn away with all the other criminals when a 'star class' prisoner passed. That is, in modern terms, a first offender. Martin wrote: I have seen the poet having to stand with his face to the wall whilst a villainous looking ruffian passed by.' Martin was a quiet hero, in effect; on one occasion when Wilde was very ill, he went to fetch some beef tea for him, and he had to hide it, so the bottle of liquid was put under his coat. On the staircase on the way back, he was stopped and told to answer some questions by the chief warder. The hot beef tea spilled against his chest, burning him severely, yet he did not give in and admit what he was doing. He later recalled that 'The hot bottle burned against my breast like molten lead.'

Martin was later sacked for giving a biscuit to a child who had been imprisoned with the adults – normal practice at the time. Anthony Stokes is convinced that Martin was placed at Reading by Haldane, specifically to care for Oscar Wilde.

Wilde, as a sensitive and cultured man, was of course, living every day with the roughest elements in the criminal class. They suffered the usual prison regime of punishment and deprivation if they erred. Flogging was still used, and at one time Wilde heard a flogging in progress on a wing landing. He was so moved and appalled by this that he wrote to the papers. The *Daily Chronicle* printed his letter. Flogging was not abolished in England until 1939, and in Wilde's day the common criticism of such a tough punishment was perhaps best expressed by Mr Justice Keating in 1874, who replied to a questionnaire on the subject, saying:

> Does it deter others? I think not: a private flogging in a prison can scarcely have that effect; to be logical, the flogging should be as formerly, at the cart's tail: yet no one can doubt that the effect of such an exhibition would be to brutalise the masses ... During more than 40 years of experience of criminal courts, I have observed crimes diminish under a steady and comparatively lenient administration of the law ...

Wilde's protests had no effect. But his time in gaol was soon over after that; he was released from Reading on 18 May 1897. His last allowance of special privilege was that he could wear his own clothes as he walked out, and that he was not in handcuffs. He then went to France, and lived at Berneval-sur-Mer until his death in 1900. *The Times* carried a brief obituary, and this summed up his tragic life as well as his rare genius: 'When he had served his sentence of two years' imprisonment, he was broken in health as well as bankrupt in fame and fortune. Death has soon ended what must have been a life of wretchedness and unavailing regret.' But they added the words that he was 'a brilliant man of letters'.

It is thanks to the fact that Wilde had such notoriety that we know so much about prison life in the 1890s, from an authentic source of a man in a cell. The other spin-off benefits for literature and history have been that Wilde was arguably one of the most talented and gifted of all Victorian writers, and that talent was forced to express the deepest and most soul searching words in his eventful life. In *De Profundis* we have a classic of prison literature and a work of rare spiritual exploration, all in the one slim volume. He may have been a 'special prisoner' but that rare case gave us insider knowledge of prison life at its worst.

Oscar Wilde's reputation since these awful events has, of course, massively expanded and today he is still more influential than he was in his life; and in cultural areas even more than in drama, in some ways. He was, without doubt, one of the most troublesome and worrying prison inmates our prison system has ever had to cope with, but that sad episode in his short life added yet another dimension to the still resonant charisma and intellect of a unique artist and writer.

CHAPTER 4

Sir Roger Casement: Hanged by a Comma

After the Easter Rising in Dublin in 1916, the British government were savage in their reprisals. The war with Germany was of course demanding their full attention, and paradoxically, thousands of Irish men had signed up and were fighting in the trenches for Britain and her Empire, when their countrymen took up arms in order to create a free Republican Ireland. After some hard fighting on the streets of Dublin, thousands were imprisoned, and in May the executions began. On 3 May, Patrick Pearse, Thomas MacDonagh and Thomas Clarke were shot in the yard at Kilmainham jail, Dublin. Other perceived leaders were shot in the next few days and then, on 6 May, no other executions were announced. Eighteen men who were scheduled to die found that their sentences were commuted, two of these being for life.

There was pressure from America. England needed her American allies to help fight the war in Europe, and Irish America did not at all like the executions. But the shootings did go on, the most disgusting being the death of James Connolly, brought out from his sick bed into the Kilmainham yard to be shot; he had been driven across the city in an ambulance, then sat on a chair in the yard, shot even though he was unable to stand. Courts-martial and death sentences continued. But a level of leniency came in, and even Eamon de Valera was saved; he had been a primary leader in the Rising, in command at Boland's Mill.

In total there had been more than 3,000 arrests in 1916, then many were released, and over 1,500 were interned in England. But one person stood out as an extraordinary case: Sir Roger Casement. He had been engaging in liaison with

Germany, and the Rising had, as part of its statements of identity and aspirations, made Germany appear like their ally. Casement was arrested for high treason and his trial took place on 29 June, the prosecution being led by FE Smith (later Lord Birkenhead). Casement's situation was bizarre and contradictory: he had taken a knighthood from King George V but insisted that his only country, his own real allegiance, was Ireland.

He had enjoyed an unbelievably interesting and adventurous life previous to his involvement with the 1916 Rising; in 1914 he had tried to create a Liberal party in Ulster, as well as his adventures far afield. But in his trial he claimed that his highest aim was to serve Ireland. He had tried to recruit an Irish Brigade in Germany, and he failed in that. In visiting the POW camps in Germany, he had been unwelcome, and as was noted at the time, he had to have a guard with him on those visits in his attempts to divert them from their duty.

Casement had gone to Germany, his movements monitored by British spies, and when he returned to Ireland it had been in a U-boat, landing off the coast of Kerry, where he had soon been arrested. His earlier life and career had been extraordinary; he had made the world aware of atrocities in the Congo and in South America, and he was something of a hero, particularly in America. He had made friends and contacts in high places. It seemed outrageous and incredible that such a man should be a traitor.

The basis of his indictment was the Treason Act of 1351 which states that the offence is defined by 'Compassing or imagining the King's death' and 'levying war against the King in the realm' but also, and this was the crucially important clause for Casement, 'adhering to the King's enemies in his realm, giving them aid and comfort, here and elsewhere'. That comma and what followed, was his death sentence. 'Elsewhere' was easily defined in a way that included activities at sea, in Germany and in fact in Ireland, so loose was the definition of the word.

His trial has been the subject of a vast literature, including an account by FE Smith himself, published soon after the events, along with other famous trials in history. Smith recalled the issue of whether or not Casement had actually committed treason, and he expressed the situation in this way: '... when I closed the case for the prosecution, the legal argument began. It was necessarily long, technical and intricate. It involved the true leaning of the Treason Act, which was originally drawn up in Norman French. It necessitated a minute examination of a number of musty statutes, long since repealed ... It was essential to grasp the details of an antiquated procedure ...'

Eventually, agreement was reached; the dates of earlier precedents in treason trials had to be noted and finally the wording which was used against Casement was 'adhering to the King's enemies'. When the sentence finally came, it was done after much deliberation, as Smith wrote: '... after Counsel's speeches and a judicial summing up by Lord Reading in terms most scrupulously fair and impartial, the jury convicted and Casement was sentenced to death'.

Casement went to Pentonville. An appeal was launched, presided over by the famous Lord Darling. The question was still there: had Casement's actions been an infringement of the law? He had been known to the public as a 'servant of the Crown' as Dudley Barker wrote. But the fact was that on 20 April 1916, near Tralee Bay, a labourer looking out to sea had seen a flashing light, and a farmer walking home later saw a boat a few yards from the shore. He beached the boat and there he found three Mauser pistols, maps of Ireland, a flash lamp and a flag. There was a jacket and in a pocket there was a railway ticket from Berlin to Wilhelmshaven. At a time of spy mania on the Home Front of the Great War, that story was enough to condemn Casement, as the owner of those materials, and as the person who had landed. He tried to claim, when the police cornered him, that he was a writer, on holiday, from his home in Buckinghamshire.

It had all been a daring and bold adventure, but now he was in court, fighting for his life. Darling soon dismissed the arguments of the appeal lawyers for Casement; he said, 'I am unaware of anything in the history of the German nation during this war which would lead me to accept with enthusiasm the suggestion that they would be prepared to offer unlimited hospitality to a number of Irish soldiers in order that when the war was over they would be able to write a new page in the purely domestic history of their country.'

Casement was asked if he had anything to say before a decision was reached and a sentence passed. He had had three weeks in prison in which to prepare a speech. His defence counsel, Sullivan, had tried to argue that no matter what a man did, at the time the 1851 statute was passed, he was out of the King's realm and so could not be tried for treason. Darling and the other judges disagreed.

Casement went back to Pentonville and just a short time before he was hanged he was accepted into the Roman Catholic church. In his time in the prison, two of his cousins wrote to the prison to ask permission to visit him and to send some clothes. The requests met with no answer, but Gavan Duffy kept fighting to have these requests accepted and considered, and finally Casement was allowed a visit. But when they did arrive there, he still had on the clothes he wore on being arrested. They had sent clothes but he had not had them. It took another complaint for the clothes to be found and then for him to put them on.

The man with the task of hanging Casement was the Rochdale hangman, John Ellis, who had executed Dr Crippen. A local man in Rochdale was asked what he thought about the Casement affair and Ellis. He said, 'Jack were very patriotic you know. He said he'd willingly give £10 to charity for the chance to hang Casement. He wer' as pleased as Punch when he got t'job. He went off to London as happy as a schoolboy.' The hangman went to Pentonville and there he went with the Governor to watch Casement, pacing in his cell; the purpose of that inspection was to ascertain the right length of drop for the man's height and weight. Ellis decided on a drop of 6ft 5ins.

On the last evening of Casement's life, a Father McCarroll stayed with him; the prisoner could not sleep and before eight the next morning he was in the chapel, and he prayed with the priest until his death at nine. This was on 3 August. Casement's last words were, 'God save Ireland! Jesus receive my soul ...' Ellis reported that Casement went to his death with great courage.

The Times reported on the end: 'By 8 o'clock a crowd had begun to assemble in Caledonian Road, which runs in front of the gaol ... about 150 people, chiefly women and children from the immediate neighbourhood, stood on the footpath and fixed

their gaze on the prison walls ... Near to where they had stood
was a group of workmen, who on hearing the bell raised a cheer.
Five minutes afterwards the crowd had disappeared and the
street resumed its normal appearance.'

The usual official notices were posted outside the prison,
confirming that the judgement of death was executed. Then
there was an inquest, held in the prison, supervised by Walter
Schroder. Gavan Duffy, a friend of Casement, identified the
body, and then asked if he could read a statement. This
dialogue then followed:

Coroner: The order for the burial is issued by me and handed
            to the governor. As to any other matter in reference
            to the burial of the body, any application must be
            made to the authorities.
Duffy: I appreciate that, Sir, I have applied to the Home
            Office for permission to have his body. I consider it
            a monstrous act of indecency to refuse it.
Coroner: On that I cannot express any opinion.

There was clearly a great deal of bitterness at the whole affair.
Duffy wanted to know whether Casement had been considered
to be insane during his time in gaol, and Dr Mander, senior
medical officer at Pentonville, said that there was no truth in
that.

What could have been more banal after that than the simple
statement that, at the coroner's hearing, a verdict of 'death by
execution' was confirmed. A petition for a reprieve had been
put together in Ireland, and after his death there was clearly a
great deal of ill feeling in his homeland.

Yet, the Casement story lives on in another dimension,
and that is related to the so-called 'Black diaries'. These diary
entries may or may not have been genuine, but the effect was to
malign Casement. The gist of them is that they show him as a
promiscuous and depraved man, and in the eyes of the public at
the time, as a homosexual: we know what happened to Wilde a
few years earlier, so the effect of that is easy to guess. The diaries
seem to have come into the possession of the government by
way of a sailor called Christensen, who was a kind of servant to
Casement. It appears that at first, the government tried to use

these entries as part of an argument to show that Casement was insane, but that was abandoned. His defence counsel refused to even look at them. There was certainly a view expressed at the time that there were advantages to Casement being imprisoned as a criminal lunatic than in hanging him and thus creating yet another martyr to the Irish nationalist cause.

CHAPTER 5

Eamon De Valera:
Sprung From Lincoln Prison

Visitors to the city of Lincoln would never be aware, unless they were suddenly taken very ill, that there was a grand and formidable Victorian prison close to the centre; it stands opposite the County Hospital, dominating Greetwell Road with its long, round-topped walls and castellar gatehouse. Opened in 1872, it replaced the old Georgian prison which was inside the castle grounds. In that long history, there have been very few escapes from Lincoln. George Brewer escaped in March 1943, to be recaptured within twenty-four hours, and in 1966 a man got free using knotted bedclothes. But by far the most notorious escapee was that of the future Taoiseach of the Irish republic, Eamon de Valera.

It was an amazing story, hitting the national headlines, and *The Times* reported the bare facts the day after – 5 February 1919: 'Hue and cry at Lincoln – Eamon de Valera, the Sinn Fein MP for East Clare, with two other Irish prisoners, escaped from Lincoln gaol some time between half past four o'clock yesterday afternoon and nine o'clock in the evening . . .' Tall and distinguished, de Valera had been a key player in the Dublin Easter Rising, being captured and imprisoned afterwards, and after spells at other prisons, was sent to Lincoln with other Sinn Fein men.

De Valera was a scholarly type, a mathematician. One of his friends at college was Charles Walker, and I have been told of a time much later in de Valera's life when Walker's text books were given to 'Dev' on a day when the famous politician invited Walker's daughter and grandchildren to tea. It says a lot about the man that he was so welcoming, but of course, his life was full of contradictions and puzzles (what politician doesn't have such complexities?). He was born in New York but raised in County Limerick by his grandmother; and later educated at University College, Dublin, joining the Gaelic League in 1904 and the Irish Volunteers in 1913. He was involved in gun-running at Howth the year after, and commanded the third battalion of the Dublin Brigade in the Easter Rising of 1916.

Before ending up in Lincoln, he had been put in Kilmainham jail after the Rising and there he expected to be shot, writing this note to Mother Gonzaga at Carysfort Convent in Blackrock, where he was a maths teacher: 'I have just been told that I will be shot for my part in the Rebellion. Just a parting line to thank you and all the sisters ... for your unvarying kindness to me in the past ...' But he was reprieved and lived to see the inside of several other jails in his long career.

He escaped from Lincoln with two other men, John Milroy and John McGarry. The description given of de Valera says a lot about him: '... aged 35, a professor, standing 6ft 3ins and dressed in civilian clothes.' The report neatly summarised the fact that tracing the men was going to be virtually impossible: 'A close search has been made all over the city, but so far as was known at a late hour last evening the escaped prisoners had not been found.' They were not the only escapees from the Sinn Fein ranks: four men escaped from Usk prison the week before.

De Valera had been arrested in the 'round up' of May that year, stopped by detectives as he went home to Greystones in County Wicklow. He was then taken across the Irish Sea to Holyhead. The forecast by journalists at the time that he would make his way back to Dublin and 'arrange for a dramatic reappearance in Irish politics' was quite right.

How did they manage to escape? Lincoln prison fronts Greetwell Road, but behind at that time was merely open ground, beyond the rear exercise yards, and to the left, along the road heading out of Lincoln, there were merely limekiln areas then. The escape was arranged so that full use could be made of the vulnerability at the rear. But having said that, there was constant supervision, and of course, they needed a master key.

A committee of Irishmen was set up to arrange the escape, and they selected a number of men to do the job. The focus was the small patch of ground used as the exercise yard; it was surrounded by barbed wire, armed warders watched in the day-light hours, and an army unit came to patrol at sunset. Sensibly, the first decision was to decide not to try a direct assault – a rush – as there would have been a gun fight. The next plan was to start by finding a way to communicate with de Valera. The answer was to use the Irish language. An Irish prisoner who was working on a garden plot in the jail sang a song, and the words gave de Valera of the planned breakout. The second time a song was sung it was to direct de Valera to have an impression made of the key that would open the back gate. Today such methods would not be possible, but then there was more work outside and so there was a degree of vulnerability with regard to the system. According to one report, the key impression was made with the snatching of a key from a warder to press it into soap, but this seems very unlikely, given the fact that the key would be on a chain and always snapped into a belt-purse when not in use. Far more likely is the theory that a prison chaplain made the impression in soap or in a bread paste. The first two keys made did not fit anyway, and then the third model worked well.

The impression was wrapped in brown paper and thrown over the wall. Then came the hard part. De Valera would be able to walk through from the main prison building, but there were the sentries to consider. They would have to be distracted, and the way to do that was to use female allure. Two girls from Ireland were used, as the local girls may well have split on them. The *Lincolnshire Echo* reported that they were 'attractive, vivacious Irish girls, both university graduates, and they were directed to flirt with the guards'. On 3 February, four cars were sent around the country around Lincoln, to create decoys and keep the police occupied, then at dusk, the Irish girls began to work on the guards. They lured them away from the prison recreation area and the Sinn Feiners then cut through the barbed wire and waited for de Valera to appear: he did, after some initial trouble. The key broke in the lock from the outside, as Michael Collins, who had come to lead the attack, tried to force it, but luckily de Valera, from the inside, managed to force it out.

They had to move very quickly, because Collins and Boland drove straight to the city railway station and caught a train to

London. But de Valera and the others split and drove to Manchester.

The conclusion given by the prison authorities about the escape was that it was facilitated by the fact that the internees were allowed to associate much more closely than ordinary prisoners, and were not subject to such close supervision. Shortly afterwards, Terence MacSweeney was released on parole from Lincoln as his wife was seriously ill.

In their time in Lincoln, the Sinn Fein prisoners were treated very well. The journal of the prison doctor records his examinations of them, and there are regular entries in that book. For a long period, several were on hunger strike, and the doctor records his comments about each one, as well as noting their weight. Paradoxically, one of the prisoners put on weight during the hunger strike – a footnote to history perhaps not widely known, and a fact that adds a humorous dimension to those troubled times.

CHAPTER 6

Her Ghost Haunts the Death Cell

Officers at HMP Hull often speak of the ghost of a woman who wanders the landings and the death cell late at night. Some have said to me, 'Oh it's Mrs Major' or 'It's Lily.' The death 'suite' still survives there, at least in terms of the rooms involved, if not the noose and the trappings of gruesome official hangings. Being there today, one can see the death cell, and then just six paces from its door to the space where the trapdoor was waiting. This is one of the 'twos' – the second level. Ethel Lily Major would have fallen down through that space, her legs kicking as she fell to her death down to the ground level – the 'ones'.

There are dozens of reasons for calling this case the most significant and contentious in the history of crime in Lincolnshire. Reappraisals of the reasons why Ethel Major was hanged for the murder of her husband when she mounted the scaffold in Hull prison a few days before Christmas 1934 have been made regularly over the years. The problem is that nothing can turn the clock back, and re-examining this case is a painful business.

The outline of the case is reasonably straightforward, but a controversy will follow. The Majors, lorry driver Arthur and wife Ethel, lived in Kirkby-on-Bain, near Horncastle with their fifteen-year-old son. They were not happily married; she was forty-two and her husband forty-four. Arthur had a drink problem and he was very difficult to live with. He also appeared to be having an affair with a neighbour, a Mrs Kettleborough, and Ethel said that she had seen two love letters written by this woman to her husband. Hard though it is to believe in hindsight, Ethel Major showed these to her family doctor and said these words to him: 'A man like that is not fit to live, and I will do him in.'

Arthur Major died as a result of what was defined as an epileptic fit, but then, before the funeral could take place, this anonymous letter arrived on the desk of Inspector Dodson of Horncastle police:

Sir, have you ever heard of a wife poisoning her husband? Look further into the death (by heart failure) of Mr Major of Kirkby-on-Bain. Why did he complain of his food tasting nasty and throw it to a neighbour's dog, which has since died? Ask the undertaker if he looked natural after death? Why did he stiffen so quickly? Was he so jerky when dying? I myself have heard her threaten to poison him years ago. In the name of the law, I beg you to analyse the contents of his stomach.

This was signed, 'Fairplay'. A coroner's order stopped the interment and Major's body was examined again. The coffin was actually removed in the presence of the mourners. Ethel was in her house with relatives, including Arthur's two brothers, when the police arrived. 'It looks as though they're suspicioning me' she told her father, and he agreed. Ethel, small, spectacled and short-sighted, was an unassuming woman with some quirky habits and a complicated nature.

It soon emerged that indeed the dog, a wire-haired fox terrier, had died after having muscular spasms. The pathologist, Dr Roche Lynch of St Mary's Hospital, Paddington, also confirmed that Arthur Major's body had the quantity of strychnine sufficient to kill the man. On examination, the surface of his body was blue, and almost any contact on the skin would initiate a spasm. Arthur's body had 1.27 grains in it and the dog had 0.12 grains. The average fatal dose for a man was between one and two grains. Lynch opined that Major had taken two doses: one on 22 May and the fatal one on 24 May. To dismiss any possibility of suicide, Lynch said, 'On account of the awful agony he would go through, I do not think that any would-be suicide would take it a second time, unless he were insane.'

It had been a terrible and agonising death. His son Lawrence saw Arthur walking into the front room with his head between his hands, then as the man went outside, Lawrence saw him fall over. He was put to bed, and when Tom Brown came later, he saw Arthur foaming at the mouth and in the throes of violent spasms. Later, when Dr Smith came, he made up his mind that this was epilepsy. It was going to be a long process of dying for the man, and in court it was revealed that Ethel had left him alone for the night, then in the following morning, she had gone shopping. Later in the day he seemed to recover and he actually drank some tea, but then there was a relapse. Virtually the last words Arthur Major spoke to his wife were, 'You have been good to me.'

Ethel Major was interviewed by Chief Inspector Hugh Young of Scotland Yard, and he has given an account of her in which she stated that her husband had died of eating some corned beef. 'She appeared over-eager to impress me with the fact that she had nothing to do with providing his meals, explaining that for a fortnight before her husband's death she and her son had stayed with her father . . .' Young was eager to point out that Ethel was a cool and resourceful woman and that she 'showed no pangs of sorrow at the loss of her husband'.

The crucially important statement made by Ethel to Young was, 'I did not know my husband had died from strychnine poisoning' and Young replied, 'I never mentioned strychnine poisoning. How did you know that?' As H Montgomery Hyde pointed out in his biography of Lord Birkett, that in Birkett's time poisoning 'was considered such a repulsive crime that convicted prisoners were practically never reprieved'.

When Ethel Major was arrested and charged, the full story emerged and Lord Birkett, talented as he was, knew that he would lose this case. There was too much evidence against her. At Lincoln Assizes, on 30 October 1934, she appeared before Mr Justice Charles. Richard O'Sullivan and PE Sandlands prosecuted, and Ethel pleaded not guilty.

One of the most convincing pieces of evidence against her was the fact that she had a key belonging to a chest her father, Tom Brown, used to store strychnine; this was used to kill vermin. Tom Brown testified that he had lost the key to his chest some years before and that he had had a new key made. When Sandlands brought out a key, Brown confirmed that it was the one he had lost. This key had been in Ethel Major's possession. There was also a hexagonal green bottle for storing strychnine; this had been found in the Majors' house. Then came further information about the access Ethel had to her father's house. She had known where a key was hidden outside, and a purse she had containing the key to the chest was confirmed as being one that belonged to her mother.

Tom Brown was questioned about this key. Here is a point of real fascination: the father was testifying against his daughter. Lord Birkett must have seen this as another nail in the coffin for his already flimsy defence. There he was in the witness-box: a whiskered old countryman. Regarding the key, the prosecution pointed out that the last key had turned up 'shining as though it had been recently polished' in Ethel Major's possession. Birkett desperately tried to retrieve the situation by saying that lots of women carried trivial objects and mementos around in their handbags. In other words, she may have had the purse and key, but not the strychnine. Tom Brown had looked at the little bottle and suggested that it seemed to have the same amount in it as it had had the last time he looked at it.

The heart of the situation was the strychnine and the corned beef she knew was her husband's last meal. Ethel had admitted that she knew some corned beef in the cupboard was not really edible and yet she had left it, saying nothing to anyone. She had known Arthur was due to eat it. Looking into the tale of the corned beef was to be important in court. Contradictory things were said about the purchase of the tin of beef; Ethel saying Arthur had sent Lawrence to buy it, and Lawrence saying the opposite. All this cast doubt on Ethel's statement, though it has to be said that the retailer recalled that Lawrence had come for the beef and said that his father had given him the money to buy it.

Tom Brown did, however, have quite a lot to say about Arthur Major's character, relating that when Brown's first wife had died in 1929, Arthur had come to the Major's place very drunk and had used threatening words. Ethel Major's daughter, Auriel Brown, was asked about the love letters and the supposed affair Arthur was having with Mrs Kettleborough. Birkett knew that if there was to be any chink in the armour of the prosecution's case, it was going to be in the possibility of provocation with regard to this affair. The focus of their dialogue was not promising in this respect:

Mr Birkett:	Did you ever see anything that you thought suspicious between Mrs Kettleborough and Major?
Auriel:	I saw them once making eyes at each other. Mrs Kettleborough was always outside the house when Major came home. She put herself in his way.
Mr Birkett:	The advances that you saw were on one side?
Auriel:	Both sides.

A great deal more information about the Majors' life together was to emerge. They hated the very sight of each other; Arthur Major had severe financial problems and he was of the opinion that his wife was a spendthrift and was helping to ruin him. Only a few days before he died, Arthur Major had placed an announcement in the local paper, the *Horncastle News*, removing himself for any responsibility in debts his wife had accrued. The situation at No. 2 council houses was far worse than many around the village would have suspected.

One fundamental cause of their rift was the fact that Ethel, before she met Arthur, had given birth to a child (Auriel) in 1914, when she was only twenty-three. She never revealed the name of the father, and the girl was brought up as a daughter of the Browns. This refusal to give details of the business infuriated Arthur; things deteriorated so much that she left him for a while, going back home to the family home.

In court at Lincoln, Lord Birkett wrote later, he knew the verdict of the jury when they came back into court after an hour's deliberation; none of them looked in the direction of Ethel Major. They found her guilty, but with a recommendation for mercy. Ethel collapsed and moaned that she was innocent as she was carried away.

There was a sure feeling that a formal appeal was a waste of time; but Birkett did join a group of lawyers who petitioned the Home Secretary for a reprieve. The response was that there were 'insufficient grounds to justify him in advising His Majesty to interfere with the due course of law'. One last ditch appeal came from the Lord Mayor of Hull, in the form of a telegram to the King and Queen, pleading for their intervention.

On 19 December, Ethel Major was executed by Thomas Pierrepoint, with the Under Sheriff of Lincolnshire present. As usual, the Governor, Captain Roberts, made the statement about the hanging being done in 'a humane and expeditious manner'.

Yet in many ways, this is only the beginning of the Ethel Major story. After all, the sentence was based on circumstantial evidence and there were certainly factors of provocation, an argument that she was not her normal self when she acted, and that there was considerable enmity and aggression towards her from her husband.

A more close and searching account of Ethel Major's life is helpful in understanding these events, and also in seeing why there have been so many reassessments of the case. She was born Ethel Brown in Monkton Bottom, Lincolnshire, in 1891. Her father was a gamekeeper and they lived on the estate of Sir Henry Hawley. By all accounts she lived a good life as a child, with her three brothers and parents, going to a small school at Coningby and then at Mareham-le-Fen. She stayed at home for some years, learning dressmaking and the usual domestic skills. But after came the liaison with the unknown lover and her pregnancy. Some writers make something of this with regard to her later criminality; it has been pointed out that of eight women hanged in Britain in important cases, five had illegitimate children. That doesn't have any real significance, but it illustrates the need some writers on crime have to find patterns and profiles.

Ethel had known Arthur Major when they were children. In 1907, he left the area to live in Manchester, but then, in the Great War, he joined the Manchester Regiment and they began to meet. When he was wounded and hospitalised back home, in Bradford, they wrote to each other. Keeping the truth about Auriel quiet until they were married was perhaps the basic error in her understanding of her new husband's personality. In court, in 1934, there was to be a great deal said about potential provocation on the part of Arthur Major, and even more written in years to come.

Birkett cross-examined Lawrence in an attempt to provide a clearer picture of Arthur Major's character traits. Lawrence confirmed that his father came home drunk almost every night and that this was becoming more severe in recent months. The topic then shifted to violence and fear:

Birkett: When he was in that state, did he quarrel violently
             with your mother?
Lawrence: Yes, if we were in.

When wife and son did retreat to Tom Brown's, they would sleep on a couch in the kitchen or in a garden shed, Lawrence sleeping in his topcoat and all his day-clothes. A story began to emerge that would, in other times and places, be part of a full picture of provocation and mitigating circumstances. In 1931, Ethel Major had taken out a summons for separation, so violent had his behaviour been. Arthur made vows to reform his life and Ethel changed her mind. Tom Brown had confirmed that 'Major used violent and filthy language to his wife and also threatened her.'

As in most marital situations of such conflict, questions will be asked about the nature of the relationship and whether or not there really was a victim and an aggressor. At this trial, Judge Charles and indeed Norman Birkett used this approach. Birkett boldly asked young Lawrence, 'Should I be right in saying that your mother all your life has been very kind to you, and your father very wicked?' Judge Charles went ahead and asked witnesses in general about where blame might lie.

Therefore we have questions such as 'What sort of a fellow was Major? and 'Did you ever see him the worse for liquor?' One could guess the outcome of this. People such as the vicar's wife and the rector talked of Major as 'sober' as far as they knew. He was a man with a very amiable public persona; yet inside his own home he was often monstrous to his own family.

If we turn to the other element in potential defence of provocation, the subject of the love letters comes up. What exactly was the truth about Arthur Major and his affair? We need to recall here that Major was many things in the village: not only voluntary work for the church but time put in as a local councillor. Ethel's report was that she found some love letters in their bedroom, and of course this has the implication that she had been searching for evidence after so much innuendo and whispering about an 'affair'. One such was this, which was read out in court:

To my dearest sweetheart,

In answer to your dear letter received this morning, thank you dearest. The postman was late I was waiting a long time for him ... I see her watching you in the garden ... Well, sweetheart, I will close with fondest love to my Precious one ...

From your loving sweetheart,
ROSE

When she faced Arthur with her new knowledge (she had already told her physician, Dr Armour) he said he would do nothing. The issue became a cause and a local crusade for Ethel; she wrote complaints about her husband to the local police and even tried to change the terms of the leasehold of their property so that she could be classed as a 'tenant'. The natural end of this was a talk with a solicitor, and a letter was drafted, as she said, on behalf of her husband, warning Mrs Rose Kettleborough not to write again. This solicitor had witnessed Major making violent threats against Ethel, but not taken it to be anything serious.

The Kettleboroughs in court provide a record of what can only be called tittle-tattle, and some of the discussion of the case on record seems entirely trivial; yet when Rose herself took the stand, there was clearly something interesting to come. In her fur coat, this small, attractive woman said that she had never 'been out' with Arthur Major. She also denied loitering to wait for Arthur by the house, as Auriel had said.

When the subject of the letters came up, Birkett tried very hard to do some amateur handwriting analysis, comparing her orthography and style in the love letters to other writing she had done. Nothing was achieved by this, and even an exploration of her past knowledge of Arthur led to nothing significant. To sum up, Birkett had attempted every ploy he could think of, but in the end, the record of the trial can be made to read more like an indulgence in small scale scandal than a murder case.

But this is not the end of the saga of Ethel Major. A study of the case by Annette Ballinger in 2000 takes a closer look at the provocation line of thought. In her book, *Dead Women Walking* (2000), Ballinger pays attention to comments made at the time about the discontent in the Major home, such as the statement by a solicitor's clerk that 'Arthur often threatened his wife. I gather that their home life was unhappy.' She also puts great emphasis on the change in Major as he drank more. His son's words that 'The drink was having an effect on my father, he was not the man he had been' do imply an almost submerged narrative that has only been re-examined closely since this sad affair came to a close.

For Ballinger, it was the issue of the right to remain silent that shaped Ethel's destiny. The factors which stood most prominently in court – the fact that the day before Major's death he had withdrawn from responsibility for her debts, and her husband's apparent condition of being a poor victim – made her silence worse. As Ballinger notes: '. . . the case of Ethel Major demonstrates how the prisoner's right to remain silent could be interpreted as evidence of guilt. Thus the judge referred to Ethel's non-appearance in the witness box no less than six times in his summing up.'

The 1898 Criminal Evidence Act had made the 'right to silence' concept very important in the construction of defences. But unfortunately, the unforeseen side-effects were that juries would tend to interpret silence as guilt in many cases. This would be despite the fact that some people in the dock would be nervous, apprehensive, or even in some cases, would have been advised by their brief to say nothing.

Ballinger sees Ethel Major as a 'battered woman' and notes that generally such women are too traumatised to give evidence. But there was no militant, prominent feminist movement in the inter-war years, of course. One common view, and this is something that helps us understand Ethel Major's situation, is that, according to Lind Gordon, 'wife beating became part of a general picture of slovenly behaviour, associated with drunkenness, and squalor of the wife's own making'.

Finally, if the notion of Ethel's failure to safeguard her reputation is on the agenda in this notorious case, then aspects of her behaviour in the village have to be an important factor in understanding how she was perceived and judged in court. Her eccentric questioning of various neighbours, her interviews with the doctor, and her letters to the press, all add up to a picture of a woman who was both desperate and indeed in a very nervous state. The documented behaviour of this woman as she worked hard to put things right in the household only made her situation worse. Of course, in court, these actions would be seen as reinforcing the moral condemnation of her as someone who had, earlier in her life, had a bastard child and not told her husband about it.

Part of the judgement on her was also that she was generally bad tempered, and this was made more prominent than her husband's equally capricious and aggressive behaviour. On one occasion she had thrown a brick and had 'embarked on a wild round of revenge and malice that included half the population of the village', according to another commentary on the case.

The executioner at the time, Albert Pierrepoint, wrote about the other way women killers need to be seen: not as the hard, rational poisoners of the media images, but as 'ordinary women, rarely beautiful ... Square faced, thin mouthed, eyes blinking behind National Health glasses ... hair scraped thin by curlers, lumpy ankles above homely shoes ...' As Annette Ballinger has said, '... poison was responsible for her death'. By that she means that the nature of that specific version of homicide carries with it a discourse and a media amplification going back centuries, as something that has entered folklore. When Ethel Major's case started covering the main pages of newspapers, the whole back-list of women poisoners was invoked. All the images of women using arsenic on husbands, from Mary Ann Cotton back in the mid Victorian times, to the earlier Lincolnshire instances, were on the stage as the sad story unfolded. For decades, the pages of the *Police Gazette* had been full of lurid tales of women poisoners; what hope was there for truth to emerge when the media had categorised them as the worst kind of heartless killers?

Alderman Stark of Hull, when he wrote a last appeal for clemency, saying 'For the sake of humanity I implore you to reconsider your decision, especially having regard to the nearness of Christmas ... The heartfelt pleas contained in this telegram are those of 300,000 inhabitants and particularly those of the women of this great city' was fighting more than a judicial decision. He was going against the grain of many centuries of myths around the 'women are more deadly than the male' notion.

The sense of defeat and the inevitable conclusion on the scaffold was hovering over her defence from the beginning. Lord Birkett's memoirs contain his view that Crown Counsel had opened with a statement that had a ring of finality: 'The case is really on the evidence unanswerable.' One of the very best defence lawyers in the land could do nothing. It seems odd with this in mind that the *Daily Express* had insisted that 'Nobody believes she will be hanged', just a few weeks before the sentence.

There was no way that an appeal based on the unfairness of the judge's summing up would succeed. Whoever 'Fairplay' was who sent the anonymous letter, he or she had opened the path to the gallows for Ethel Major, and the only consolation, looking back over the years, is that the Pierrepoints were very skilled men in their trade. Ethel would have left this world very speedily indeed, though they must have felt something similar to John Ellis when he hanged Edith Thompson in 1922: 'My own feelings defy description ... I kept telling myself that the only humane course was to work swiftly and cut her agony as short as possible.' This is a stark reminder of what feelings were with James Berry when he dealt with Mary Lefley.

Unfortunately, in spite of all the above discussion of this fascinating case study, the reference books will always have the same kind of simplified statements for the record, as these words from Gaute and O'Dell's *The Murderers' Who's Who* (1979): 'Major, Ethel Lillie, a 43-year-old Lincolnshire gamekeeper's daughter who murdered her husband with strychnine.' The woman who never gave evidence at her trial is being judged by posterity, still enveloped in silence. In modern terms, and with a more feminist, open-minded view of *mens rea*, the mind-set to take a life, it can be argued that in 1934 there was a too narrow definition of intention, because the accused is supposed to see the same probability that the jury do, in the way that the intention is given to them by lawyers interpreting the defendant's actions.

But all that would have been far too subtle for the court in Ethel Major's case.

CHAPTER 7

Lord Haw Haw: Germany Calling

William Joyce, alias Lord Haw Haw, was a problematic case from the start. He had broadcast propaganda to Britain in the Second World War, and so he had incited hatred and fear. Was that traitorous? He definitely had an impact. I can recall talk of him in my childhood in the 1950s; my family all knew of him and the aunts and uncles could all imitate his cut-glass voice. In effect, he had infiltrated the British consciousness. Hitler wanted to undermine morale, and he found the right man for the job. Some found the broadcasts genuinely unnerving, while others scoffed at them.

Whatever the opinion we have of Joyce might be, with hindsight, at the time he was very much a wanted man, and he became as troublesome a prisoner as he was an enemy existing purely on the air, rather than in the field.

Joyce was an American citizen, born there in 1906, and after that he was in Ireland until 1921. He moved to England until the outbreak of war, and then he moved to Germany. Within a few weeks of that move he was employed to broadcast from various stations in Germany. He had obtained and used a number of passports, and that became the issue in court that would decide whether he lived or died.

He did have an effect: the BBC conducted some research into this in 1940, and they found that a significant proportion of the population listened to Joyce's broadcasts regularly. 750 people filled in the BBC questionnaire, and over half of them said that they listened because it was entertaining. Surprisingly, 29% said that they thought the broadcasts would give the German view of the war – a credible one. The subsequent report said, 'If there were widespread discontent . . . this would be Hamburg's opportunity. The impact of Hamburg propaganda should be kept under proper observation.'

Joyce was captured by two soldiers, Captain Lickorish and Lieutenant Perry, near Flensburg on the Danish frontier. Even then Joyce was projecting a false identity. He had a German passport and was stated to be called Hansen. At first he spoke French, but then English, and his voice was so distinctive to the English ear that the officers knew it was Lord Haw Haw. He reached into his pocket and, as the officers suspected he had a gun, was shot in the thigh. As he dropped he said he was Fritz Hansen.

Joyce had given various conflicting accounts of his life and birth over the years, and when he appeared in court, the defence had to argue that he was not a British citizen and so could not be tried for treason. The statute in question was created in 1351 and the important wording there with regard to treason is in these statements: 'Compassing or imagining the King's death,' and 'Adhering to the King's enemies in his realm. Giving them aid and comfort elsewhere.'

What darkened the waters of the case even more was Joyce's letter, written to the officers' training corps at London University, in which he said: 'I am in no way connected with the United States of America, against which, as against all other nations, I am prepared to draw the sword in British interests. As a young man of pure British descent, I have always been desirous of devoting what little capabilities and energies I may possess to the country which I love so dearly ...'

We can imagine the difficulty with which Sir Hartley Shawcross in the Central Criminal Court asked the jury to forget all previous knowledge and formed opinions of Joyce so that the case could be heard fairly. He said to the jury: '... Some of us formed feelings of dislike and detestation at what he was doing ... and some of us heard that he had been arrested and brought to trial. If any of you had any feelings of that kind about this man, I ask you, as I know you will, to cast them entirely from your minds.' He was asking the impossible. The man had been a celebrity – someone to joke about and imitate while at work or in the canteen.

Joyce's passport was issued, renewed in 1939, and then his quick departure was bound to go against him. A document was made available that showed he had more than likely arranged for the employment in Germany before leaving. Nevertheless, he was forthright in his denial of having been a traitor. He wrote: 'I know that I have been denounced as a traitor and I resent the accusation as I conceive myself to have been guilty of no underhand or deceitful act against Britain, although I am able to understand the resentment that my broadcasts have, in many quarters, aroused.'

He was sentenced to death, by Mr Justice Tucker, and then his appeal was heard before the Lord Chancellor, Lord Jowitt and four other lords. The verdict was succinct:

> An alien who has been resident in but has left the realm may be convicted of high treason in respect of an act done by him outside the realm if at the time of the commission of the act he was still enjoying the protection from the Crown as to require of him continuance of his allegiance. The possession of a British passport affords such protection.

The fact is that, to the world in judgement of him, Joyce appeared to want to be under the protection of several states. The decision was made after discussion of the distinction that 'protection' was the protection of British law, not a de facto protection, 'such as might be enjoyed by a person who possessed a forged passport until the fraud was discovered.' Of the five judges, only Lord Porter was in support of a reprieve.

Joyce's wife, Margaret Cairns Joyce, came for a short visit to the condemned man, and was then returned to an internment camp in Germany, and then later released to live in Cologne, where she was subject to an appraisal by the de-Nazification Board. His brother, Quintin, also visited, and wife and brother saw him separately.

Joyce was a 'celebrity' prisoner of course. A man who had been a media star was clearly expert at rhetoric and was never short of the right words for the occasion. He made one last statement for his public:

> In death, as in this life, I defy the Jews who caused this last war, and I defy the power of darkness which they represent. I warn the British people against the crushing imperialism of

the Soviet Union. May Britain be great once again and in the hour of the greatest danger in the west may the Swastika be raised from the dust, crowned with the historic words 'You have conquered nevertheless.' I am proud to die for my ideals; and I am sorry for the sons of Britain who have died without knowing why.

He was hanged on 3 January 1946 in Wandsworth, by Albert Pierrepoint and Alex Riley. A crowd of 250 people had gathered outside and the usual notice was then posted, stating that the death sentence had been carried out, and the inquest returned the verdict of 'Death by judicial execution.' But behind that plain statement there was a horrific story. Back in 1924 Joyce had been attacked by a gang at Lambeth baths in Battersea and a razor had cut him deeply across one cheek. It took a hospital stay of two weeks before he could walk out into life again, and he did so with a massive scar across the face. He had been given twenty-six stitches. When it came to the time when Albert Pierrepoint had to hang the man, the scar burst open and blood spilled onto the prison floor. He was buried, according to custom, beneath the stone floor of Wandsworth. The corpse was thrown on top of another body, a murderer. It is interesting that in Pierrepoint's autobiography, there is no mention of Joyce.

History is all about perspectives and stances taken on the past: a feature written in 2005 concerned Joyce's daughter, Heather. On the day her father was hanged, she went to teach English at a convent school in St Leonard's on Sea. She went with her students to watch a war film and everyone was laughing. When interviewed in 2005, the report states, Heather said she could not recall that film but, 'That day is burned in her memory. She was carrying a secret, burying it so deep inside her that, when she started to talk about it years later, it dominated the rest of her life.'

Joyce's spell in gaol and at execution still created a stir after his death. The appeal hearing was discussed at length in the press, and one writer, Lennox Russell, writing a year after the hanging, pointed out the odd sequence of events leading to the quashing of the appeal: he noted that the appeal was dismissed on 19 December, and that a plea to the Home Secretary was then rejected on 2 January (the day before he hanged). On the same day, Lord Porter's disagreement about the appeal court decision was reported. Russell wrote: 'Was the Home Secretary in possession of them [the documents relating to the appeal] when he rejected the pleas for mercy? Or had he before him no statement of the views of the final court of appeal, or only some statement other than the one published?'

Russell had spotted something very odd. He added, putting the issue very clearly: 'The case was one ... in which it was peculiarly desirable that there should be no possible ground for any suggestion that the accused had not been given the benefit of any doubt.' He saw a problem in procedure, and people reading between the lines must have wondered whether there were reasons, expressed by Lord Porter, for clemency, which had not been aired publicly, and certainly not in the press reports. The execution, some argued, had been totally contrived.

One coda to the Joyce story which is interesting is the fact that it was he who coined the phrase 'The Iron Curtain.' In one of his addresses, called Views of the News, he had said, 'The Iron Curtain of Bolshevism has come down across Europe.' This was broadcast from Hamburg in April 1945. Many things in his life had been odd, accidental and puzzling. Even his nickname was created by a writer called Jonah Barrington, and it was supposed to be given to Norman Baillie-Stewart, another broadcaster from Germany. He then gave the name to Joyce after being sent to the Tower for treason.

CHAPTER 8

A Spy and a Rogue in the War

The two notorious prisoners figuring here present two real extremes: the first comes across almost as a figure from a semi-comic adventure story, but at the time he was a real threat to home security. The second is an incredible story of a conman and killer.

What were the internal security forces to do about Germans in Ireland in 1939–40? The place was clearly seething with Republicans who would stop at nothing to find willing allies in the fight against the Brits. There were Germans there, and in quite large numbers, some pretending to hunt for butterflies or to stand in awe looking at the magnificent beauty of the cliffs of Moher or the Dingle. They didn't want to be, in the words of Noel Cowards' song, *Beastly to the German,* who might be genuinely spending time in Ireland for study or for holidays; but then, it became clear that there was skulduggery afoot and that something had to be done. After all, they were up against spies who lifted weights, loved philosophy and even – Heaven forbid – enjoyed a romantic novel.

Military intelligence scrutiny of neutral Ireland in 1941 was becoming far more intensive, after a period of tolerance and observation, waiting for developments. One event, a parachute drop into Ireland in March 1941, was to be sensational, and not a little entertaining. That is because the German spy in question was undeniably a 'character'. This was Gunther Schutz. The Irish Section of MI5 was dealing with a mass of paperwork at the time, following all kinds of leads and reports, but they did manage to have the man arrested almost immediately.

Schutz was not the smartest pencil in the box. After the drop, he managed to have his suitcase radio found, and had not succeeded in hiding it anywhere. He was found wandering around near the village of New Ross, County Waterford, by two policemen. His radio and a roll of notes were found in his case, and he said he was Hans Marschner. In the notes made on him by army intelligence, we have some details that add to the impression that he specialised in dramatic failure: 'It was a lovely night, and the clouds and distant mountain flooded in moonlight made the most beautiful sight he had ever seen. Then houses and trees began to rush upwards against him, and he landed, stunned with nose bleeding, in a field.'

The next stage after his arrest was to subject him to inter-rogation, and the man for that job was Richard Hayes, recently attached to the Irish Secret Service, who had drafted in his kids to help unravel the German Abwehr code.

Schutz tried desperately to be someone else. After 'Marschner' he told the tale of his being a South African living in London who liked flying and parachuting for a hobby. He must have thought that his German and vaguely English intonation sounded like a South African accent. In fact, the address he gave in London was indeed a place used by Abwehr agents. This safe house, at Webster Gardens, was under surveillance. It had to stay apparently 'safe' though, and the front was preserved, something crucially important as a very important agent known as Rainbow had been located there, and it was learned that Schutz had made contact with him. In fact, the man who landed in the Irish field had lived for some time, posing as a student in London, attending the Commercial School in Ealing. He had a talent for study and would have done very well there. He had already done missions in Spain and at the Abwehr base in Hamburg. The man who on the surface assumed shambolic was perhaps a major player.

Schutz's presence in Ireland now became much more impor-tant for MI5. The real clue as to why he was an important arrest was in the fact that he had a microscope – meaning that he was able to access a new type of coding that used microdot patterns. The question was, how best to watch this man and make the most of his presence in Ireland? The answer was in Mountjoy prison in Dublin, because that was where the German internees were held, and it seemed virtually certain that Schutz would be able to attempt some kind of communication there.

There had to be German spies in the establishment at Mountjoy in Dublin as well. From September 1939, it had been recognised that the Abwehr and the IRA would be potentially a very dangerous alliance. There had even been links between the Abwehr and Welsh nationalist extremists. Warning signs about the types of espionage legends that were created by the Germans were available, as in the case of a man called Ernst Weber-Drohl who was arrested in Ireland and so he was released by the court, having insisted that he was not a member of the Nazi party. His narrative was that he had been a fairground entertainer, known to the crowds as 'Atlas the Strong' and was a minor celebrity.

Schutz was placed in Mountjoy and watched closely, having been given a seven-year sentence and put first in the gaol at Sligo, and later interrogated and thoroughly searched at Arbour Hill prison, Dublin. He had the habit of reading magazines and novels clearly in genres meant for feminine reading; *Just a Girl* seemed to be his favourite, and that was almost certainly the code book for his operations. This was a book by Charles Garvice, a novelist of the Edwardian years who had a major hit with *Valentine Vox,* an equally romantic work of torrid affairs and secret desires. He was in some ways the quintessential spy – even having liquid for secret writing in his clothing-pads when thoroughly searched. But *Just a Girl* was to turn out to be very ironic, in his prison escape. In your average prison community, a guy reading such popular literature would be in danger of receiving unwanted sexual approaches, but in Schutz's case the approaches were more standard undercover brainwork. The system of microdots worked on a basis of him picking a certain page to encode that would link to a specified day of each month.

Prison work and the basic security measures enforced in a prison regime involves a keen sensitivity to any matter pertaining to clothes and dress, as in the instances of such things as prison drama productions where wigs and disguise might be worn. For obvious reasons, sanction for such things would have to be very carefully considered and then, should clothing be granted, the vigilance needed to check for misuse would be very acute. The very idea of a prisoner wearing a wig, for theatricals or even Christmas festivities, is enough to give a prison governor sleepless nights and nervous twitches. But the governor in 1942 allowed the prisoner the purchase of a set of women's clothes, supposedly to take home to his sister.

He was having a hard time generally, mixing with the lags, thugs and wastrels known in the city as gurriers and gutter types. He hated being treated like a con and he would request some distinctly literary and very high-culture reading, such as a complete Shakespeare and Dante's *Divine Comedy*. One hardened old gaolbird robbed him of his watch and another, a tough nut called Anderson, threatened him and abused him whenever he could. He had to find a way out of the place. One ex-con is on record as saying, 'That German fella read more love books than my missis.'

But in 1942 he had managed to acquire a saw and he cut through bars, made it to the outer wall along with a Dutch prisoner called Van Loon, who was caught in the grounds before he made it to the wall. The escape was organised by some IRA prisoners, and amazingly, Schutz spun a tale about the women's clothes to the governor, saying they would be a gift to take back home to his fiancée after the war. It is hard to imagine the scuttling figure of a man in drag running through the streets of Dublin, jumping at every shadow, particularly as he was moving alongside the Royal Canal in areas where the ladies of the night were seen at their trade. We could speculate on whether or not he could have coped with the subtleties of the English language if approached by a potential customer who thought he really was a Dublin woman looking for some business.

However it was done and he went into the city after scaling the wall; the fact was that Schutz escaped and the intrepid spy was housed with Irish politician and soldier, Cathal Bruha's widow, Caitlin. Schutz had even been given detailed maps of the city and information on known safe houses. He had the sheer hutzpah to write a letter from the Bruha house to Caitlin's daughter, who was also interned, and true to form as a dashing but stunningly feckless type, he wrote, 'How I do miss you every evening when the paper comes, I mean the crosswords, without your assistance it is a hell of a job, I can assure you.'

There was a wanted poster out for him, 'Hans Marschner', issued by the Garda, with a substantial £500 (worth over £14,000 today) reward, and there is a small photo of him: a dapper, well-groomed man of about thirty who could easily have been a film star on a Wills cigarette card. He is described as '5ft 9ins, complexion pale, hair dark brown, scar between eyes and on left cheek. Speaks English well.'

But he was recaptured there and then taken to Arbour Hill gaol. Most of the German spies were returned to their homeland in 1947 after a spell in an internment camp in Athlone. It can only be assumed that he spent most of his war years reading the great writers, doing crosswords with the women internees and ordering more books by the inimitable Charles Garvice, a writer who, in spite of his phenomenal success in romance, has not the smallest mention in *The Oxford Companion to English Literature*.

The second story is the tale of a consummate, many-sided crook who made his own impact on the war – and on his victims.

He was the quick-change artist of fraud, the epitome of Shakespeare's line that 'one man in his time plays many parts'. He was a one-man danger zone for everyone who met him, a ladies' man with the manner of a cultured gentleman and the morality of a death-camp torturer. By 1946 he was to be a multiple murder, but in the war years, he committed fraud and deception more than any other crook. His name was Neville George Clevely Heath, a man who always had money, savoir-faire and grudging admiration, but was destined for the death cell where he was desperate to leave his last few pounds to his young brother.

In the course of the war, Heath was to be an officer, commissioned in the South African Air Force, and a dozen other people, largely because being in a uniform attracted him like a toy shop window for a child. On the surface, he was that stereotype, the plausible rogue, but deep down there was the personality of a psychopath – but one who acted the role of fatal charmer.

This glittering career of fraud and murder began early, but so did the dark, evil killing instinct. He was only just prevented from raping a girl at a party when he was in his teens, something that amazed his family; his mother said of him, 'Like most boys, he was always bright and full of fun and though he knew lots of girls and might keep changing them, he has never had any trouble with them as far as I know.' But this was the boy who put his hand over the mouth of a girl at a party and tried to ravish her.

He was born in middle-class Wimbledon in 1917 and he went to a good school where he excelled at sport. He was always an impressive rugby player and athlete, but he was not academically bright, and when he left school he took a job as office-boy at Pawson and Leaf, a firm in the City of London. But that was tedious for him and the lure of the uniform and fast cars was too much for him; he managed to get a short-term commission in the RAF, after a spell with the Artists' Rifles. He was just seventeen when he went to Cranwell for training, and it is on record that one officer said of him that 'This man has the makings of a first-class pilot and should prove himself an officer with outstanding abilities.'

There was no doubt that Heath could fly a plane: he always had the knack of being able to fly any kind of craft. But his criminal mind showed itself at this early stage when he began to spend far more money than he earned and he decided to embezzle the Mess funds when he was Sports Officer in Duxford, Cambridgeshire. When the officers of No. 73 Fighter Squadron gathered for discussion of the subject, Heath was missing. He had written a dud cheque and his squadron leader rang him up to ask about it, but he went on the run, stealing a car belonging to an RAF sergeant, which he left abandoned on Waterloo Road, London. Of course, he was dismissed from the Service, though found not guilty of desertion.

After other crimes, he went on the run again, and a detective cornered him and he was arrested. At the Old Bailey he was sentenced to a spell in Borstal for counterfeiting a banker's draft. There he was, a man who thought he was an officer and a gentleman, at a Borstal for 'Boys'. It was the ultimate humiliation for him. After some time in Wormwood Scrubs, he was sent to Hollesley Bay, at Woodbridge in Suffolk, and there, with 400 other boys, he returned to his life of charm and play-acting. The boys were allowed to wander out into the village and with servicemen. He would mix with officers and their wives, being able to talk about his 'RAF career' framed by lies and stories. But he managed to join the Army Air Cadet Force and told tall tales about flying Lysanders and about almost being killed on daring raids. He made it to second lieutenant in the cadets and then, in an era when checks on career histories were very slack, he managed to get himself attached to the Army Air Force Co-operation Unit in March 1940 and was posted to the Middle East.

He was, of course, very popular in the mess in Palestine, and even as a 'one pipper' lieutenant he had the charm and wit to ingratiate himself with his senior officers. There was a general there who wanted to sell his car as he had no use for it when on active service, so naturally, Heath agreed to buy it, but it was simply to re-sell it and make money. He thought he would make a lot of money, because he paid for the car with another dud cheque. Heath was sure that it would take a long time for him to be found out, but he was wrong, and the general came looking for him, in a rage. At his second court martial he led his own defence and things could have been worse: he was merely cashiered.

Going home to England was out of the question, so Heath hopped on a boat and went to Durban. The lure of the uniform was still strong in him; he would have considered being a hotel commissionaire if need be, just to wear the uniform. But his air force days were not over, and with the assumed name of James Robert Cadogan Armstrong, he joined the South African Air Force. They were impressed with both his flying skills and his prowess on the rugby pitch and he was sent to Transport Command. It was here that his dreams of grandeur and affection for living as an impostor began to flower, and he took another name, Bruce Lockhart. That was the name of the famous traveller and spy, and one of the real Bruce Lockhart's friends told Heath he was a liar. The episode tells us all we need to know about the man: he said he was using the name to deceive the enemy because he was actually in the British Secret Service. He told the man he was really Captain Selway of the Argyll and Sutherland Highlanders.

He was utterly joyful to hear that he was being posted to England, and soon he was in Oxfordshire, and he could resume his life of fraud. Here he became 'Jimmy Armstrong', a persona he made into what can only be described as a 'war celebrity'. But he was found out. He returned to South Africa, married and had a son, and then of course, he was back in court again, in Durban. For the third time, Heath was dismissed from His

THE HISTORY OF NEWGATE

LONDON: A. RITCHIE, RED LION COURT E.C.   COMPLETE   PRICE ONE PENNY.

The History of Newgate, from 1890. (*Author's collection*)

Florence and James Maybrick.

The entrance, inside
Marlborough Street police
court, where Oscar Wilde
appeared. (*The author*)

Reading Gaol in 1848, from an old print. (*Author's collection*)

Detail from the *Lincolnshire Echo* newspaper report of the De Valera escape. (Lincolnshire Echo)

WHEN DE VALERA ESCAPED FROM LINCOLN GAOL

ECHO ————◆———— 19.2.48

Defeated in the election for the Premiership of Eire by five votes, Eamon De Valera to-day looks back on 16 years spent as Prime Minister of his country. Perhaps his mind goes back further to the turmoil of the Easter Rising, to the troubles of 1919 and to his imprisonment in Lincoln Gaol.

Picture of De Valera taken shortly after his escape.

IF those are his thoughts to-day he will no doubt live once again those hectic hours in February, 1919, when, with two comrades, he escaped from prison, was whisked away to London and was soon back in his own country.

The story of the escape reads like a thriller, with the singing of songs conveying messages in code, an impres-

∧ ∧ ∧

"BECAUSE of this military force it was decided that it would be unwise to try to rush the place for fear of loss of life and the possibility of De Valera being killed.

"The next move was to communicate with De Valera—a very difficult matter. But one Sinn Feiner started working on an allotment near the prison and attracted the leader's attention by singing a Sinn Fein song in

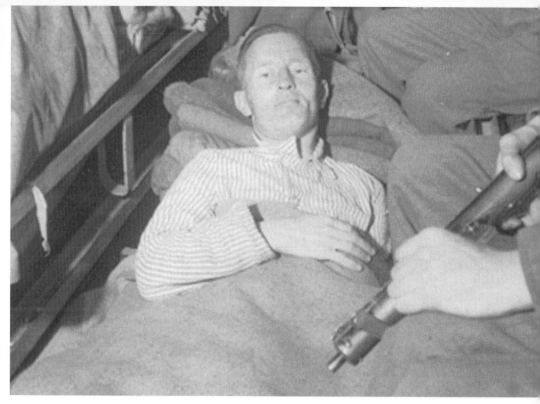

'Lord Haw Haw' under armed arrest.
(*Author's collection*)

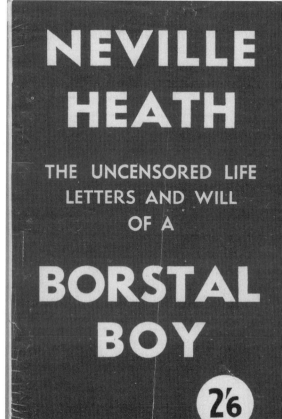

Cover of the first biography of Neville Heath
by Gerald Byrne. (*John Hill*)

Ruth Ellis.
(*Author's collection*)

The *Magdela*, where Blakely was drinking before his murder by Ruth Ellis. (*Vicki Schofield*)

Killer 'made two tunnels in attempt to escape'

From Our Correspondent
Winchester, March 22

Harry Roberts, who killed three policemen, made two attempts to tunnel to freedom from the maximum security wing of Parkhurst prison, Isle of Wight, it was stated at Winchester Crown Court today.

When the first tunnel was discovered he was transferred to another cell. There he dug the second tunnel, using identical construction and concealment methods for each one.

The disclosure was made by Mr Bernard Wilson, principal security officer of the maximum security block, at the trial of Mr Roberts's mother, Mrs Dorothy Roberts, aged 73, a widow of Augustus Street, Camden, London.

She has pleaded not guilty to smuggling bolt-cutters into the jail on November 30 with intent

Extract from *The Times*, 23 March 1973, on Harry Roberts' tunnel.
(The Times)

A portrait of Dennis Nilsen. (*Vicki Schofield*)

The box: evidence from Nilsen's flat of body parts.
(*Vicki Schofield*)

HMP Durham where Staffen was observed. (*Author's collection*)

The Blind Beggar, where Cornell was murdered. (*The author*)

A scene after the Hull prison riot of 1976. (*HMSO*)

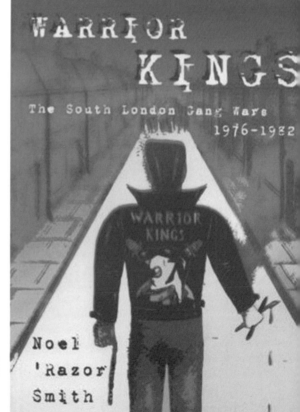

Cover of Noel 'Razor' Smith's book, *Warrior Kings*. (*Apex Publicity*)

Majesty's forces, given a military escort to the docks and put on a ship for Britain. A man who knew him in Durban said Heath was 'The cocktail party type seen wherever it was fashionable to be seen.' But back home, his sinister side came out and he was in his own personal mythology, 'Jimmy the Ripper'.

It is almost certain that his first murder took place in South Africa in 1943. He had been divorced and had had a lot to drink, and Heath drove off for a ride in the country with a young woman. He came back alone. The story he gave was that the car had burst into flames and he had tried to put it out, but that he had jumped from the car, then ran after it to try to save the girl, but that she had been burned beyond recognition. There was an investigation, but the Devil's luck was with his protégée, and Heath was never charged.

The number of his victims in wartime London and elsewhere will never be known: some were raped, others robbed, many were ripped off with bad cheques and tall stories, but deep in his personality, Neville Heath was also a sadistic killer. He was more dangerous to women than arsenic-laced foundation cream. Heath met Margery Gardner in May 1946, when he had been living under a succession of assumed names, roaming and roving the country looking for casual (and very violent) sex, but also for a lifestyle of pretence, fantasy and dangerous delusion. This love of hotels and hot sex was to lead to his first known murder: Margery Gardner liked unusual sex as well, and at the *Pembridge Court Hotel*, London, the woman's screams from the bedroom were heard by the hotel detective. There was nothing illegal found out and no prosecutions, but Heath, after proposing to another woman, returned to that hotel with Margery later, and this time he left her dead; she was found by a cleaner lying naked, on her back, with her ankles tied together and with several scourge marks on her body. Heath had used a whip with a diamond pattern and this was seen on her flesh.

Heath killed again: he murdered Doreen Marshall, whose body was found in bushes at Bournemouth, naked except for one shoe. Her throat had been cut and she had been beaten; one nipple had been bitten off and there were severe cuts on her body, from the vagina upwards. Some object, possibly a branch, had been pushed up her anus. He was caught and charged, and in court an insanity pleas was given, but this was to no avail and Neville Heath was sentenced to hang.

The fantasist and turned killer, and the man who had entertained thousands with his tales of wartime heroics and persuaded the world that he was a professional sportsman as well as a bomber pilot, was in Pentonville prison in October 1946, when the cell door opened and the hangman, Albert Pierrepoint, made sure that Heath was quickly pinioned, taken to the noose and hanged. He was hanging more than the pathetic and evil man in that cell – he was killing Major Jimmy Armstrong, Captain Rupert Brooke, Prisoner number 1059 – and Jimmy the Ripper.

CHAPTER 9

Mutiny in North Yorkshire

In the years following the end of the Great War in 1918, many prisons were closed, and in 1922 HMP Northallerton in North Yorkshire ceased operations, though the buildings were left standing by. In the old tradition in Britain of utilising existing establishments when new necessities arise, when war came along in 1939 the place was in use again, this time as a training depot for the military police. The cells provided accommodation for the trainees, and from a mere store it was transforming into a busy military location.

In the early days of the Second World War the military police comprised all kinds of personnel, from the Auxiliary territorials (women) in the service to the elite such as the 150 Provost Company, whose men took part in the 'Phoney War' with the British Expeditionary Force in 1939 in France; in that action, there were numerous thefts of stores and equipment and a Special Investigation Branch was formed. But for most officers in the military police at the time, routine duties were such things as the enforcement of order and discipline, instructor work, record office clerical work or security duties. But there were different kinds of military police: the Red Caps are of the Provost Wing; the Traffic Control Wing work by particular areas; then the Vulnerable Points Wing guarded important sites and installations. Clearly, the latter group were the Northallerton deployment.

For a few years at the outbreak of war, then, these men had special training for those duties; though destined to become the Royal Military Police in 1946, in those first years they had an important but routine set of duties on their agenda.

In 1943, it was needed as a prison once again and became a military detention centre. There was to be a radical transformation in the next few years, as the prison changed from a place where soldiers would be trained for such things as the prevention of sabotage at important sites to a military detention centre. By 1946, Northallerton became national news, though not for good reasons. It was the location of a mutiny. To tell the full story of what became known as 'The Glass-House Mutiny' it is necessary to place the events in the context of that year.

In the House of Commons, on 26 March 1946, Mr Lawson, Secretary of State, responded to Tom Driberg with regard to an enquiry into conditions at Stakehill Detention Centre near Bolton. This was the report in *The Times*:

> [Lawson] said that he had recently received the final report of the Court of Inquiry into conditions at Stakehill Detention Barracks. The general conclusion was that the allegations which had been made in the public press and in letters to the Rev.Urien Evans, or to members of Parliament, were either unfounded or grossly exaggerated. The Court of Inquiry, which included among the members a KC and a psychiatrist, examined every aspect of the problem in great detail. Every effort was made to call as witnesses all those who had made allegations about the treatment of prisoners at Stakehill, and also all soldiers under sentence who had any complaint to make. They examined in all 195 witnesses including 47 members or ex-members of staff ...

It was all very thorough, but his conclusion – that 'there is no need to make any further enquiry into conditions at Stakehill' – is very much at odds with personal testimony from some sources, and this evidence enables us to take a less than sanguine view of the kind of prison conditions which were to affect Northallerton severely.

If we set beside Lawson's words this extract from a memoir, *I Couldn't Paint Golden Angels,* by Albert Meltzer, we are led to re-think these matters. Meltzer was an anarchist who had already done a stretch in Brixton before he was sent north to Stakehill:

> Stakehill had hit the news because a prisoner had been found dead. The Church of England chaplain is usually in such circumstances a minor administration official but in this particular case an enthusiastic young parson objected to

the guards declining to take their hats off when escorting prisoners in church. He protested but to no avail. Then one day he was down in the detention cells and heard cries. He rushed in to find that two warders had just hit a man who was lying on the floor. One of them was saying to the other, 'Kick him staff, he's still breathing.' When the horrified padre asked what had happened, the other staff sergeant said, with an equal heavy attempt at jocularity, 'Don't mind him, Sir, he's always lying on the floor, crying.'

Meltzer wrote that he found the place 'seething with mutiny'. He saw that something was deeply wrong, and he noted that many of those being abused were 'a credit to the nation'. He pointed out that the cruelty was often extreme: 'Yet for some minor infraction of absurdly imposed regulations or breach of discipline ... we were kept in cages. It was Brixton gaol all over again but more so.'

At the same time, Aldershot military prison experienced severe problems: this was on 23 and 24 February and that was to spread to other gaols, including Northallerton. What happened at Aldershot was that a detainee managed to smash his way out of his cell and release others in the hall where he was kept; they overpowered the NCO and gathered more men as they went on the rampage. The Commandant addressed them with a loud-speaker and used threats of severe reprisals but this had no effect. Troops surrounded the block where the men were, and the mutineers took to the roof. There were around forty men involved and their rage of destruction lasted well into the next day.

Some of the men involved there were recently arrived from Northallerton, as it was reported at the time: 'There seems no doubt that the disturbances were a development from a frustrated attempt by six soldiers under sentence recently trans-ferred from Northallerton, and were not a generally concerted act of mutiny.'

In fact, Northallerton was to see the same thing, just a week later. On 1 March rioters there forced their way into one of the prison stores and set fire to it. Some of the men climbed onto the roof and began throwing bricks. The local fire brigade arrived and put out the fire. The rioting took place in a hall holding seventy men, but exactly how many were involved is a matter of conjecture. They were long-sentence prisoners and things were in a condition of extreme danger: armed soldiers from Catterick camp were called in and a cordon was placed around the block. There had been two earlier incidents and the first was the one in which the men sent to Aldershot were involved: in the first riot there was considerable damage done to buildings. Sixteen men had escaped after morning church parade on that occasion. A week later another sixteen men broke down the gate through which the earlier escape had been attempted. The use of a hose-pipe put paid to the latter trouble.

In the main mutiny, what happened was that the out-break was confined to the one barrack; officers and managers acted quickly and efficiently; the rioters could not get near the armoury. Of course, there were some serious repercussions. An officer was hit by flying slate. But there were no escapes. The War Office official announcement said:

> The trouble appears to have been started by nine prisoners transferred from overseas on February 26. The mutiny was confined to some of the men in one block only. Men under custody in the other block and in Nissen huts were not involved. Fifty troops from Catterick have arrived to reinforce the barracks staff, but the situation is now under control except that about nine men were still on the roof at 5 p.m.

The leading lights in the insurrection were from the British Army of the Rhine. The main source seems to be a unit which had served in Italy and the disaffection that began there was carried with them back to England. The Secretary of State made a speech in which he hedged around the whole area of what underlying grievances might have been. The main one was that sentences for quite minor offences were very long, as Meltzer had claimed in his memoir. The Secretary bluffed and spoke vaguely, saying, '... it is clear that some of the soldiers under sentence, some of whom have criminal records, were in a mood to take full advantage of the opportunity to join in this act of mass indiscipline.'

In Northallerton, the papers created a narrative of high drama and dramatic incidents. The *Daily Mail* photographer managed to take a flight over the prison and to take a shot showing all the events: he labelled the picture to show the hose being used against a man on the roof; he showed the positions of all the fire brigade installation, and made sure that his readers would be reassured by seeing the armed guards placed around the gaol. The same paper later printed a shot of the destruction, with the caption: 'Two pictures from a Daily Mail cameraman who visited Northallerton (North Yorkshire) military prison during yesterday's riots, when long-sentence prisoners seized the main block of the gaol, smashed everything they could, and set fire to the Army stores.'

The *Mail* main headline said it all: 'National Glasshouse Plot Suspected'. It was a case of hype on a grand scale; unfortunately, in the years since then, there have been exaggerations and distortions. One account states that 'two regiments' were needed to quell the riot.

The end of the mutiny was described in the *Daily Express* on 2 March, in these words from Reginald Butler 'inside Northallerton prison':

Seven long-term prisoners, bedraggled and shivering – they had been drenched by hose-water for hours – climbed down from the rafters of this military prison at 7.45 tonight after a roof-top siege which lasted eight and a half hours. So ended an all-day riot involving nearly 300 soldiers – less than a week after the disturbance at Aldershot, Glasshouse No. 1.

Butler went on to say that 'most of Northallerton's century-old prison was wrecked' – which is clearly grossly inaccurate.

Naturally, there was a trial of the mutineers. The evidence suggested in their defence was that their commanding officers in Europe had indicated that the men would only receive a short sentence, and that was very wrong. The men had originally gone AWOL after serving well in the theatre of war; their sense of injustice is not difficult to imagine. On 27 April, it was reported that eleven of the soldiers were charged with mutiny and faced court-martials at Catterick camp. The men were from the Pioneer Corps, the Royal Scots, the Royal Northumberland Fusiliers, the General Service Corps, the Seaforth Highlanders, and (most ironically) from the Loyal Regiment. The men were named and shamed in the national press.

CHAPTER 10

Ruth Ellis:
Crime of Passion

The reading public know a lot about Ruth Ellis, the blonde killer of her lover; the desirable West End hostess who went through failed relationships; we even know, thanks to the television series, *Most Haunted*, that her spirit is reckoned to haunt at least two locations. The fact that she was the last woman hanged in Britain is also something lodging in the general consciousness. There have also been several media portrayals and, most famously, the film on her life and crime in which she was played with great power and impact by Miranda Richardson. But the very last piece of documentation on her could not be more horrendous and disenchanting.

The document is the post-mortem report on her from HM Prison, Holloway, in July 1955. That report states that she was 'well nourished, with evidence of proper care and attention', and that she was 5ft 2ins, with a weight of 103 lbs. The summary of the corpse after hanging was simple, technical and direct:

> Deep impressions around neck from noose with front of the angle of the lower jaw. Vital changes locally and in the tissues beneath as a consequence. No ecchymoses [discoloration from ruptured blood vessels] in the face, or indeed elsewhere. No marks of restraint.

She had been dead for an hour when the pathology was done. Her spine was dislocated, and there were fractures in the oesophagus. The pathologist, the celebrated Keith Simpson, added 'Deceased was a healthy subject at the time of death. Mark of suspension normally situated ...' One little detail indicates much about her life: 'Lower abdominal operation scar for ectopic pregnancy.'

Her life and the murder she committed are well known, but we need to summarise that here before looking at her prison life and last days. She was born Ruth Neilson in 1906, the child of a professional musician, Arthur Neilson, in Rhyl. Her father had worked on the liners which left from nearby Liverpool, but when that industry declined the family moved to Basingstoke, and then, in the War, to Southwark. Ruth was just fifteen when she started work in a factory but was too ill to continue so in her enforced period of unemployment she learned to dance. She was, from the start, gregarious, lively and always longing for some glamour in her life.

The first step on the road to being a club hostess was when she worked as a photographer's assistant. That work entailed some work at the dance halls. In the great age of the jazzy dance bands, she was dropped into the heart of the club culture and she loved it. Ruth's first failed relationship was with a Canadian called Clare; she became pregnant and he went back home: a pattern reproduced across the land when the soldiers were, as the saying has it, 'Over sexed and over here'. The child was born: Andria Clare, in September, 1944.

One clear way out of her mess was to try modelling and she found some work: at just nineteen she met Morris Conley. Known generally and in the media as 'Britain's biggest vice boss.' Working at Conley's business, the *Court Club*, she met the alcoholic George Ellis and he was very much infatuated with her. He persisted in his attentions, and he offered her some stability and financial security, and so they married and settled in Southampton. Then again, the relationship failed. Ruth was back in London after a few years, working for Conley. She was promoted in 1953, becoming the manager of *The Little Club* in Knightsbridge. The job had perks and a good salary. But a regular customer, David Blakely, met her and soon they were living together.

She always had plenty of admirers, and arguably the one who really loved her was Desmond Cussen, who was rich and generous. But Ruth's wild side longed for what Blakely could offer: excitement, fast cars, drink, parties and life on the edge. When she became pregnant, Blakely's dark side came out: he beat her up and hurt her so much that a miscarriage was caused. A few days later he brought her flowers and they were friends again. That familiar pattern, so often observed in domestic violence, was the bedrock of what would later be the spur to murder.

After saying that he would meet Ruth for drinks with their friends, the Findlaters, Blakely did not appear: he had left with the Findlaters to join them in a party somewhere else.

Blakely was drinking in *The Magdala* club, Hampstead, with his friend Clive Gunnell. They came out, laughing and joking, to Blakely's car, a Vanguard, parked outside. Ruth was waiting for him. Blakely had ignored her, stood her up, and of course she had welling up in her the hatred and resentment of a long period of abuse. She had in her hand a .38 Smith and Wesson revolver. Ruth called his name and Blakely just went on shaking his car keys; she called again and as he turned she shot him twice and he staggered around the car. Three more bullets were fired into his body at close range. Then one more shot was aimed down at the pavement. Ruth's spree of death and damage was still not done though: a passer-by was shot in the thumb from the ricochet of the shot.

At her trial, Melford Stevenson really only had one gambit for the defence: the fact that she was so upset that there was a case of diminished responsibility. If he could show that she was out of control, and indeed 'demented' then he might save her neck. But she was doomed. She was sentenced to death and had an appointment with Albert Pierrepoint, the publican-executioner.

Off she went to Holloway to await the outcome of an appeal. She had not wanted to launch an appeal but her lawyers did so nevertheless. A letter was sent to the Home Secretary, but as the appeal went on, Ruth merely wanted to die. She tried to persuade her brother to smuggle a drug into gaol so she could take her own life. He refused. She had time to spend in prison, and she read the Bible, quoting to visitors the Old Testament law of 'an eye for an eye and a tooth for a tooth'.

Her thoughts were naturally on Blakely, and she asked her friend, Mrs Dyer, to go and see Blakely's corpse, so she could report back. Apparently he was lying in a satin-lined coffin and Ruth was satisfied he was well cared for in death. She also wrote to Blakely's mother, saying, 'I implore you to try to forgive David for living with me, but we were very much in love with one another. Unfortunately David was not satisfied with one woman in his life.'

In prison, she was generally composed and self-controlled. Her biographer, Robert Hancock, writes that she was managing the days before her death by doing what she was good at, 'playing a part'. He says, 'When she appeared at the Old Bailey, she knew she would be a national figure. The fame that had unfairly passed her by so far was hers now. Ruth Ellis was not going to let Ruth Ellis down by any sign of weakness.'

In Holloway she read thrillers, as well as the Bible. That says a lot about her and her dual nature. She had been brought up a Roman Catholic (though there was Jewish ancestry) and that was still in her character. She and the men she cared for had certainly gone through ordeals and hellish suffering. Her husband, George Ellis, had taken his own life in a Jersey hotel. He was on record as saying about his wife, 'I was frightened to death of her. She was ruled by a passionate, uncontrolled, insane jealousy.' Those words needed to have been spoken in court, but Ruth never wanted an insanity plea. A doctor who examined her at that time reported, 'She indignantly denies that her behaviour of the weekend was hysterical ... her whole history is that of an emotionally immature person.'

There is a whole library of books on the hanging of Ruth Ellis. Attacks were made on the verdict, and it was all about the legal procedure around the trial, with the basic condemning question left out of the picture. That question had been:

Mr Christmas Humphreys:	Mrs Ellis, when you fired the revolver at close range into the body of David Blakely, what did you intend to do?
Ruth Ellis:	It is obvious ... when I shot him I intended to kill him.

It took the jury only fourteen minutes to decide on a guilty verdict.

Ruth spent twenty-three days in the condemned cell at Wandsworth. That was a long wait, giving the press and public plenty of time to agitate and express themselves. There was an appeal for clemency. When Pierrepoint and his assistant, Royston Rickard, arrived the night before the execution, to observe the client, and to assess weights and drop measures, the crowd outside was very noisy. Hundreds of people were at the prison gates, singing hymns. Some rushed and battered at the prison gates. Extra police had to be called in.

Pierrepoint worked out the necessary drop as being 8ft 4ins. Then, early in the morning, they chalked the spot where Ruth would stand and placed the noose. As they were doing this, she was writing some letters, and finally wrote an apology to Blakely's mother. She would have been sitting there wearing canvas underclothes, compulsorily directed for women, but otherwise she was not in prison clothes in her last hours. The last hour was somewhat extended when a phone call was received, supposedly a reprieve from the Home Office, but when this was checked out it was proved to be a hoax.

When the time came, Pierrepoint only had to take Ruth a few yards to the gallows: the process was very sharp and professional, both hangmen working to pinion her and tie her legs, then Pierrepoint shoved the lever for the trap.

Ruth Ellis in her prison life is still something of a mystery. At one point, some papers on her were stolen from a store inside the prison. Her biographer wrote, in 2000, that 'In December 1967 a prisoner at Pentonville prison told the authorities that the missing papers might be in the hands of a man who ran a club in Hammersmith, who planned to sell them in the USA. They are still missing.'

CHAPTER 11

Harry Roberts:
1966 And All That

The list of those prisoners whose prison term stretches across several decades are very few. Britain's longest serving prisoner, John Straffen, died in 2007 after being inside the big house since 1951. Not far behind him in the dire statistics of isolation is Harry Roberts, the killer, along with two other men, of three police officers in 1966.

A lifer in jail has to accustom himself to more than a routine: that word comes nowhere near the sheer depressing experience of years of confinement within a circumscribed space. The pad becomes the central personal space, and that area of eight by twelve feet becomes a microcosm of flat, oppressive selfhood. The gym or the chapel become welcome respites from the company of yourself. Memories have to be erased by sheer force of will. Dreams and nightmares will be your own business and mostly will never be related to anyone else. What staves off the will to end the isolation is the creation of rituals. Small rewards and even smaller anticipations become dominant. Sharing a coffee with someone who might listen to a fragment of your experience is a major event.

For a lifer, the sense of self implodes; many develop habits of cranky, obsessive thinking and write interminable letters to the national prison newspaper, *Inside Time*. A recent newspaper called *Context* encourages a reading culture of complaint and querulous argumentation on minutiae. Lifers relish that outlet. Harry Roberts has had this for decades and he is surely now as familiar to prison officers as their morning mug of tea and the roll call when there are movements across the establishments.

Who has thought of Harry Roberts in that great gap of time? The point of such a punishment for such a heinous crime is obliteration of the self. He has become a non-person. His life, in a massive sequence of huge moments, chained into his small, diminished daily events, has moulded into one great stretch of time, one seemingly endless moment.

Yet he has not been forgotten. In fact his name and story have reached into popular culture. One reason for this has been Jake Arnott's novel, *He Kills Coppers* (2001) in which the writer fictionalises Roberts' life in some aspects. Roberts has entered the popular narratives of football, because the chant: 'Harry Roberts is our friend, is our friend/ Harry Roberts is our friend/ he kills coppers/ Let him out to kill some more, kill some more/ Let him out to kill some more, Harry Roberts.' This was first spoken after Roberts' arrest, by people outside Shepherd's Bush police station. He is something of a hero in anarchist circles, and that chant will provoke the authorities wherever it is sung.

For years now, Roberts has been a familiar face in all kinds of contexts: the craggy, dented face looks out at the world without emotion: it is so much the face of a villain and a tough that it sends up its own image, just as has happened in the case of Myra Hindley's mug shot. Harry Roberts' mug shot is a definitive one – it defines the whole genre of 'hunted man' images.

The facts of his crime are very simple: he and two other men were driving in Braybrook Street, East Acton, when they were stopped by three officers in an unmarked 'Q'-car. The policemen, PC Geoffrey Fox, Sgt Christopher Head and DC David Wombwell were shot dead. Roberts killed two of the officers. The patrol car, Foxtrot Eleven, had stopped near to Wormwood Scrubs prison, so there was some suspicion about the three men loitering there. When the blue Vanguard car of Roberts, Witney and Duddy reversed towards the 'Q' car, a check was made on the plate. The killings sorted out that problem for the gang, but after they ran and panicked, Witney was soon traced after the car was seen in Lambeth. John Duddy had dashed up to Scotland, and he was picked up in Glasgow.

At the trial, Witney's evidence was on the grounds that Roberts had frightened and bullied him. But all three were given the life sentence and the thirty-year minimum term.

The Roberts story became a saga after he ran into hiding. He was an ex-soldier and was skilful in survival skills, so he went under cover in the country. For three months he was in hiding, until he was caught in a barn at Blunt's Farm near Bishop's Stortford. He had taken risks, such as travelling on public transport and going shopping at times; but he had never been identified by the public and in the end was found quite by chance.

He was sentenced to life imprisonment with a minimum period of thirty years. He was twenty-five at the time, having been born in 1936 in Kennington. As I write this, he is still inside. His prison life has been eventful to say the least. In 1973, while in Parkhurst prison on the Isle of Wight, he made two attempts to tunnel his way out. After the discovery of the first tunnel he was taken to another cell and there he dug a second tunnel. All this came out during the trial of his mother, Mrs Dorothy Roberts, after she had allegedly smuggled bolt-cutters into the prison. At that trial, a security officer, Bernard Wilson, revealed the tunnels story.

This trial was at Winchester, and the defence counsel was the famous novelist and playwright, John Mortimer, who described the escape features and methods: 'The hole in the wall had been disguised by a thin board painted to match the cell wall in each case.' The mystery is that spins (cell searches) were done every two weeks, and Mortimer guessed that the tunnels would have taken several months to dig. The officers must have been fooled by the *trompe l'oeil* of the wall feature. The barrister suspected that there would have to have been some kind of collaboration or 'turning a blind eye' by someone on the staff, and Bernard Wilson agreed with that possibility. In fact, Mortimer asked, 'Was there an absolute breakdown in prison security?' The officer did not deny that.

Roberts had been a busy man and had been working on a major project – one which could easily have given him the use of tools and materials. He was, said Mr Victor Easen, making a two and a half foot power boat and that had kept him busy for eighteen months. It is common practice to use shadow boards for tools in prison, and there are also strict controls over the kinds of tools and artefacts used in pads; it is obvious that Roberts found ways around these measures, and his boat build-ing was just what he needed as a ruse, a distraction, and as a source of tools for the real work in hand. Unbelievably, as *The Times* reported:

> Mr Roberts had a full set of carpentry tools at his disposal. He said it was unlikely there would be a pair of bolt-cutters in the tool chest. Twenty people might have been in a position to use the washroom key.

As to the bolt-cutters, Easen told Mortimer that these could have been brought by another visitor. One possibility was the wife of Jack McVitie, the man killed by Ron Kray, she used to visit the maximum security block. Easen said, 'A blind eye was turned at the end of her visits when she used to kiss and embrace. She was visiting a man called Green and was his common law wife. The jury were asked to believe that the bolt cutters could have been passed across on one of those occasions. It seems unlikely.

Mrs Robert pleaded not guilty to aiding her son to escape from the prison; Victor Watts, prosecuting, said that Harry's mum had worn a fur coat and trousers when she visited on 30 November. It was commented by one officer that staff had never seen her wearing trousers. We have to ask what kind of searches were done on visitors at the time. Bolt-cutters down the leg of a pair of jeans would have been spotted in the most cursory search.

Regarding the planned tunnel, a piece of plywood was found over the hole, and the list of other items found is beyond belief: a pair of sun-glasses, a compass, a pair of wire-cutters, a dinner knife, a wooden brace and some drill bits, newspaper cuttings with maps of the Isle of Wight, screwdrivers, a file and some bank notes. The bolt-cutters would have been used to cut through the security fencing at the jail. When Mortimer examined an officer, Mr Duffield, on the matter of the smuggling, the man said that searching at that time was not thorough. He said they were short of staff and that 'Mrs Roberts was not searched properly on 30 November . . . We try to be humane over visitors and give people as long together as possible.' He had no knowledge of anyone searching Mrs Roberts' bag.

That was not the only surprise for the court. Mortimer said that the cutters could have been left in a washroom and then found by anyone – staff or prisoner. An officer responded by saying that a control console would have shown when a wash-room door was opened. He said 'It would have been an unusual occurrence and the control room would have reported it.' That fact had never been mentioned before at the trial, apparently for security reasons.

On 29 March 1974, Mrs Roberts was found not guilty. The jury at Winchester Crown Court was out for over five hours.

For her book, *Killers* (2003), Kate Kray visited Harry Roberts in Gartree High Security prison. She had met him before, back in the late eighties. She therefore was clearly surprised at how well he still seemed now, in his seventies: 'Harry was waiting for me, fit and well and dressed in the usual prison 'uniform' of sweatshirt, jeans and trainers.' He set about controlling the interview and restricted his talk to the main events of the crime, rather than any kind of personal exploration of his life.'

Roberts the prisoner had done what many do: cultivated the brain. He had become a Mensa member and had been obviously devouring what interested him in the prison library. Kate Kray took from him a rich, detailed account of his prison escape, including one story of him making a crossbow but needing some elastic. He told her that a woman knitted tank-top jumpers for prisoners, with a length of strong elastic in them which could be taken out.

Roberts had seen the inside of a prison before the murder. In 1959 he had been at the Old Bailey, charged with robbery with violence after breaking and entering a home, pretending to be the tax man. He was given a seven-year stretch and was told that he was 'a brutal, vicious thug'.

In his existence as a lifer with a real life term, he has done what many do: enter the world of the artist, and learn the essential skills. He paints, and Kate Kray was impressed, although there is one drawback: he tends to draw murders of police officers. He has clearly indulged his artistic skills in a number of ways, one being making pastries. He is apparently skilful at making pastry flowers. This is all very much in line with the typical prison arts product and activities found across the establishment: many prisoners paint watercolours or make impressive matchstick vehicles, create computer art or edit magazines of poetry. Harry Roberts is in that category. But as a prisoner there is clearly still one fundamental problem: he still lives up to his chin in the thoughts and imaginings of his high-profile murder, back in the year when England won the World Cup.

CHAPTER 12

Dennis Stafford: Escape from Dartmoor

t is hard to believe, but there have been several escapes from Dartmoor prison. As Trevor James wrote in his book, *About Dartmoor Prison*, 'Throughout Dartmoor's history every escapee has had to face the hazards on the moor, a vast expanse of barren heath and bogs and rocky tors.' He adds, 'Every trick you ever heard of has been used by determined men breaking out from Dartmoor. Convicts have dug down through floors, prised stones out of their cell walls and even managed to hack their way through the barred windows, using makeshift ropes to lower themselves to the ground.'

In the late fifties and early sixties of the last century, there were six men 'gone away' within a few months, and one of these was Dennis Stafford. Stafford and William Day escaped on 5 January 1959, after using an improvised ladder, a pole taken from some scaffolding. There may have been outside help. *The Times* reported: 'The search was made difficult by heavy rain and a thick mist over the moor. Even those familiar with the area often missed their way. In places a car's headlamps could only penetrate a few yards. Immediately the escape was discovered, Devon County Police put their escape plan into operation. Rings of foot and motorised police around the prison spread for 20 miles.'

Stafford was something of an expert at escaping from Her Majesty's hotels. He had escaped from Wormwood Scrubs in November 1956 and then recaptured in Trinidad. His career on the wrong side of the law was eventful to say the least, as he had also had damages awarded against him for causing a road crash in which a young woman had died.

But the real impact of Dennis Stafford was to come later. The inmates of British jails who have been interviewed about Dennis Stafford agree that here was a man with a lively mind – he liked chess and good conversation. Some report that, despite all this, there was something in his eyes when you spoke to him that showed he had an inner toughness. If ever a man needed such strength, it was this son of Joe Stafford. This is because his life has been a creative mix of myth, sheer media hype and undoubtedly a story of a miscarriage of justice.

The myth and the media are easily explained – Stafford is the man whose life inspired the cult crime novel and film, *Get Carter*. He is now seventy-seven. It is astonishing, when we read the compelling narrative of Stafford's colourful life, that he is not yet the subject of a minor genre of crime-writing, with its own following.

The basis of the major story in Stafford's life is the Sibbett murder: the circumstances are dramatic and atmospheric in the extreme. The sheer extent of the consequences, reaching into both tragedy and farce, make this one of Tyneside's most notorious and intriguing cases. On a snowy night in January 1967, Angus Sibbett's body was found, full of bullets, on the back seat of his Jaguar in South Hetton. He had been a collector in the one-armed bandit business in that area for some time, and it is now known that he was creaming a huge sum of money for himself from this activity. According to Frankie Fraser, the figure was around £1,600 a week (about £24,000 today). His offence was certain to make enemies and put his life at risk. Sibbett was living a jet-set lifestyle. His boss was Vincent Luvaglio, known as Vince Landa, and his son Michael played a prominent part in the set up, some say. The affair was later to be known as the 'Gaming Wars' – a reference to the film, *Get Carter*.

But what really happened on that night of murder in the snow? Ironically, a whole troop of miners walked past the car and none of them reported seeing a corpse inside – some even recalled a hand coming out of the window to wave them on. The likely time of the killing was between 11.15 pm and 5.30 am. A Jaguar in that place would have been something so unusual that it would certainly have been noticed. This did not tie in with the official police report.

Stafford and Michael Luvaglio were not together for the whole evening, only for a period of just forty-five minutes. The prosecution insisted that, in that short period, the two men followed the victim to the lonely place where his body was found, shot him after ramming the car, and then travelled like Stirling Moss back to Newcastle to be seen at the Birdcage Club. The problem with this was that there was no forensic evidence. The arm from the car was seen at a time when the police were saying that Sibbett was dead on the back seat. The blood that was actually found inside the Jaguar was not blood that matched any of the people involved – not even the victim. There was also a notable bias in the trial, some have argued, with the judge referring to the accused as 'Brutus and Judas'.

The accused had pleaded not guilty and the prosecution, led by Henry Scott, insisted that there had been painstaking forensic work to establish their guilt. Scott's summary of events was that the car had been found with its radiator damaged and the lights and windscreen wipers switched on. The engine had seized up. There had supposedly been a collision involving this car and the accused's car and five bullet cases were found which apparently matched the bullets in the Jaguar's bodywork. The other car involved was also said to be a Jaguar, and it was alleged that green paint from the accused's car was found on the bonnet of the red one owned by the victim, Sibbett.

In this way, a set of circumstances and 'facts' was assembled to make the case look like a clear-cut one, with a gangland killing at the centre. Reading the reports of the case today, after noting that it took the jury three hours to find both men guilty, it has to be said that Stafford's track record on the wrong side of the law was a determining factor. According to crime historian James Morton, his father, Joe Stafford – he was born Joe Siegenberg – was a man who acted as a 'straightener' in the London network. That is, he would be involved in negotiations with the law to sort out bail payments and build an 'account' with certain clientele. Not only did Dennis Stafford have this family connection; he had lived a life of high adventure that makes him seem like someone from a James Bond story.

Stafford had been the managing director of a buying agency in Trinidad after escaping from Wormwood Scrubs at the age of only twenty-three. He had been doing a seven year stretch for possessing and receiving stolen goods and there was a break-in charge as well. On coming home to see his family, he was re-arrested and made an appearance at Newcastle for further crimes. But even more startling was the Dartmoor escape. When he and Day escaped after serving six months, Day drowned during their escape journey, although Stafford had tried to save him. He was recaptured and was later freed, in 1964, coming north and being mixed up with the Landa empire.

The campaign for a retrial, because of what was seen as Stafford's wrongful imprisonment, was long and intense. In 1969, just after the trial, it was noted in the press that the evidence had been only circumstantial and that Stafford had challenged the police to prove that there was a motive and indeed a witness. Stafford has always been insistent that there was evidence which was never produced at the trial. Bits and pieces of this were to emerge gradually as the pressure was maintained. In 1972, for instance, *The Times* reported that Mr Justice Croom-Johnson was hearing the evidence of witnesses in open court. Many of these witnesses never appeared at the original trial, of course, and hence the stink around the whole affair. A highly unusual legal procedure began as transcripts from these new witnesses were collected and sent to the court of appeal. This could only be done because of recent legislation passed in the Criminal Appeal Act of 1968, which modified the original 1907 Act.

In 1972, no less than nine witnesses stated that the Sibbett Jaguar was not damaged at the time covering the first hours of the day, as it lay near the railways bridge and the mine. Some witnesses now gave their times of viewing the car as being between 3 and 3.40 that morning. This was more than two hours before Sibbett's body was found in the car. There had even been a sighting by a witness who saw the Jaguar outside her house in Beech Grove, Newcastle, at 12.10 that night.

Stafford and Luvaglio were sixteen miles away when the killing took place and there they were, at the time of the appeal, serving twelve year sentences. Something was sadly and outrageously amiss here. There was more sensation at the hearing when the pathologist, Dr Jack Ennis, denied that he had changed his evidence. This followed a statement by another doctor – the one who certified the death – that the body was showing signs of rigor mortis at 6am. Ennis had said that death occurred between midnight and 4am. This muddle could only add more confusion and uncertainty to the situation.

By 2002 it seemed that there was some kind of resolution and closure of this unique case. Strasbourg decided that, by refusing Stafford parole, Home Secretary Michael Howard had breached his human rights. After all those years inside and caught in a net of frustrating legal combat, Stafford was paid around £28,000 in damages. In 2004, new guidelines on full-life tariffs were introduced and the law has generated a vast and unwieldy machine to monitor full-life sentences and parole procedures. The Criminal Cases Review Commission has shown that justice is eventually possible even in the most convoluted and long-lasting cases – Timothy Evans, the man wrongfully hanged for one of the Rillington Place murders, was declared innocent.

David Lewis and Peter Hughman wrote *Most Unnatural,* an enquiry into the case published in 1971, to raise awareness, and that played an important part in the resolution. Yet the name of Dennis Stafford will evoke debate, disagreement and legal dispute as time goes on. It will go on reverberating through the North East in particular whenever the phrase 'One-armed bandit murder' is spoken. The question remains – who did kill Angus Sibbett?

In March 2009, Stafford and Luvaglio met in order to play their part in a judicial review of the case. Stafford told *The Sunderland Echo*: 'The problem was that Michael Luvaglio wasn't the sort of person you would take on in a pillow fight, never mind to kill his best friend.' The same paper has labelled Stafford 'The Playboy Crook' – and that seems like a back-handed compliment.

The tall tales and misleading statements go on. Only as recently as June 2009, Gordon Witton told Durham Crown Court that Dennis Stafford had told him that he was guilty of the Sibbett killing. Stafford commented: 'I am hardly going to tell an ice cream dealer that I am guilty.' Taking a long view of this case in crime history, it has to be said, with some frustration, that it is time the myths and exaggerations stopped and a real closure was reached. But whatever the reasons for the mystery and the ongoing questions, one thing is sure: Dennis Stafford has been high in the ranks of notorious prisoners.

CHAPTER 13

Dennis Nilsen:
Nice To Be Loved

here is an old African proverb that says, 'When an old person dies, a library burns down.' That applies to wisdom, but it also applies to the mystery of a human mind. At death, there is little doubt that Dennis Nilsen's demise will be like a library burning down, but it will be a macabre location of murder and the stink of corpses.

Nilsen's name is firmly entrenched in the dark library of works on serial killing; his name is in all the lurid collections at the more popular end of the true crime spectrum. He was arrested for the murder of fifteen people in 1983 and has been languishing behind bars ever since. Prison is for retribution in most eyes, but it is also for public protection, and if ever there was a man from whom the public needed protection, it is Nilsen.

Yet there are paradoxes, as there always are with psychopaths. The man himself and the crimes he committed are like two compartments in a train, separate yet part of the same construction. He is lodged in Full Sutton high security prison as I write this, doing what lifers do: read, take part in various useful and creative projects, and live with thoughts and memories which will forever hook into their surface selves, like parasites. Since being inside, he has been occasionally busy in print in various places, but he has also, controversially, written a long autobiography, and that will not, as far as the case is now, see the light of day.

Before looking at his time inside, we need to recap on what exactly his crimes were. This has often been told, but the essential facts are necessary. He was born in November 1945 at

Strichen, Fraserburgh, Scotland; his mother is Scottish and his father Norwegian. His parents were divorced in 1949, and Nilsen's grandfather, of whom he was very fond, died when Dennis was only six.

He was in the army between 1961 and 1972, being a cook in the Catering Corps; serving in Yemen, Cyprus and Germany. When he left he joined the police and then the civil service. In London, he committed his first murder – of Stephen Holmes, strangled with a tie. Between 1978 and 1983 he killed fifteen young men, and was sentenced to life imprisonment in 1983. One of the unusual aspects of his life since then is that he was involved in a televised interview from prison, in 1993.

As with all lifers, his case is subject to judicial reviews, and in 2003 the issue of his autobiography was raised. It is called *The History of a Drowning Boy,* and after a failure in court in Britain, permission to publish is still a matter held in the limbo of human rights' decisions. In 2006, he was denied any further parole applications. He has said, 'I am always surprised . . . that anyone can be attracted to the macabre. Their fascination with types like myself plagues them with the mystery of why and how a living person can actually do things which may be only those dark images and acts secretly within them.' Certainly in the extremes of deviant psychology there is the fascination with what *homo sapiens* is capable of doing. The definitive work on Nilsen, *Killing for Company,* by Brian Masters, has a title which suggests an answer. But what Nilsen did was first allure gay victims by charm and conversation, then spend time with them, being sociable and amiable; and finally he throttled them and cut their bodies into pieces. He sometimes boiled their heads. His handiwork now features in the Black Museum at Scotland Yard.

How can this behaviour be explained? In court, the defence argued from the testimony of two psychiatrists, Dr James MacKeith and Dr Patrick Galwey. They stated that he had a troubled childhood, and had difficulty expressing his emotions; the result was a shaky sense of self and an inability to have responsibility for anything. Galwey put a label on the killer: he had 'False Self Syndrome' which includes an element of schizophrenia.

In October 1983, Nilsen admitted to killing fifteen men. *The Times* reported:

Mr Nilsen, aged 37, showed the police where he had hidden bodies under the floorboards of his North London flat before dismembering them and burning the remains or flushing them down the toilet ... Mr Green said that Nilsen admitted not knowing how many bodies there were under the floor because he had not done a 'stock take'. He told the police he had killed the victims with his own ties, adding, 'I started with about 15 ties. I have only got one left.

The psychiatrists were certainly kept busy. One report announced that he had sexual fantasies, tended to have black outs brought on by alcohol abuse, and had a grandiose craving for attention. The opinion was that the victims had died because they ignored his lonely outpourings when they were in his flat. His fantasies involved his being naked and unconscious. He had said to Dr MacKeith who was analysing him, when talking of his victims: 'If they entered into it, it would be okay. If they slept they would be dead! You have got to listen to me. I am a valuable member of society. Once they were dead, I would stop thinking at fever pitch. It was the ultimate to pay for apathy.' On one occasion, Nilsen had taken his dog for a walk and he was carrying the internal organs of victims in a bag. One conclusion about his mental state was expressed in terms of an element of schizophrenia, but one doctor said that Nilsen clung to the routine of office work and union activities 'as though drowning in his own nightmares and to try to reassure himself and others that he was not the grisly monster that in ordinary language he is'.

As with numerous high-profile trials for homicide through the ages, the question was whether or not Nilsen knew what he was doing and whether he had the intent to murder. Dr Paul Bowden had interviewed Nilsen and at trial he said that Nilsen was manipulative and was indeed aware of what he was doing when he took lives. The judge backed up Bowden's thinking and on 3 November 1983, he said that this was a case in which there was some mental illness, but that there was a solid argument in favour of *mens rea* – the intention to commit the crime.

The jury were not as sure. Finally, the judge agreed to take a majority verdict and Nilsen was found guilty on six counts of murder.

As a prisoner, Nilsen is undoubtedly notorious, but this has been, in recent years, more related to issues of creativity, expression and human rights. He, like most lifers, has become very much an expert with language, having had time to read, think and absorb all kinds of information. I have known lifers who have studied foreign languages, set themselves the task of reading all the world's literary classics, or started philosophy courses and become experts on Plato or Marx. Nilsen writes to the prison newspaper, *Inside Time*, and one of his recent letters has been about the case of a scrapped issue of that newspaper after a contentious article was published, having a drawing of a pig, which was perceived as anti-Moslem. Nilsen wrote: 'Those of us of a certain age are well acquainted with the word "appeasement" and, I guess, one would have had to look very hard indeed in 1934, after the "Night of the Long Knives" in Germany ... to see a cartoon in the papers of a pig with a Hitler moustache and wearing a swastika armband ... criticising the encroaching fascism of that time ... When intimidation works, then we either stand against it or meekly await its next and more exorbitant demand!' This could be a letter from a university academic. The vocabulary and the grammar are impressive and the whole expression very powerfully and skilfully done. The Nilsen who killed for company is hard to locate.

In his prison life it has been in the matter of words in which he has caused a stir. His autobiography runs to 400 pages. This was written while he was in Whitemoor and he managed to send it to a publisher. But the manuscript has been seized and kept from him. The case is whether or not he has the right to publish the book, and in the High Court in 2001 Mr Justice Elias said that Nilsen could be allowed to challenge the decision to withhold the book from him and not to allow publishing. Although the proceeds from the book, as Nilsen has said, would go to charity, the issue is really about the content and the treatment of the crimes as in the narrative.

In March 2002, he lost the legal battle. The High Court decided that the Prison Service had the right to seize and keep the typescript and indeed to work on it to censor material.

Creative writing in prisons provides the opportunity for prisoners to express themselves in a variety of ways: they may choose to join drama groups or poetry workshops. But one tempting option is to write their autobiography. Many dream of writing a best seller, thinking that their life of crime would have the same kind of appeal as the 'red back' true crime books on the shelves, concerned with gangland and hit men, drug trafficking and bare-knuckle fighting. Recent successes in publishing crime memoirs have increased that interest. But the Prison Service is ruled by the order preventing the activity of writing for profit and also prohibiting any writing that deals with offences the person has committed. Nilsen was up against the latter, which is why he stated that any profits would go to charity.

Nilsen's lawyer, Flo Krause, insisted that the government, in suppressing the book, were breaching Nilsen's human rights under article 8 of the European Convention on Human Rights. The breach was arguably against his 'family life, home and correspondence' as it was worded in the Act. She also argued that article 10 was breached: this concerns freedom of expression. Mr Justice Crane rejected the plea, saying that 'The Home Secretary is fully entitled to require that the manuscript be stopped and read.' The only argument the lawyer could try was that the book was 'a serious work about his life and imprisonment'. But his case had not been helped by the fact that, back at the time when the manuscript was completed, Nilsen's lawyer had taken it out of the prison.

In 2004, the topic was in the news again. At the Court of Appeal, the case was turned down. The judges agreed that the script 'Glorifies the pleasure that his crime caused him.' They added, 'We do not believe that any penal system could readily contemplate a regime in which a rapist or murderer would be permitted to publish an article glorifying the pleasure that his crime brought . . .' The general opinion for some time had been that the script did not offer serious comment about imprisonment, but was an indulgence in the nefarious past of the man.

Then, in 2006, there was more to come from Dennis Nilsen. He wrote a letter that reached the press, and in that he wrote about his crimes and about the autobiography. It was sent to Tim Barlass of the *Evening Standard*, because Barlass had been in touch with Nilsen for a while. Nilsen wrote about his book: 'My own autobiographies have been obstructed and banned by the Home Office, every inch of the way. A whole list of writers, journalists, and independent academics (some from the US) have wished to visit me in prison, but all such applications have been rejected by the (mostly) Labour administration ... Under Straw, Blunkett, Clark and now Reid, as the Stalinist Red Flag keeps flying, if not in the past then presently in their minds when it comes to censorship.'

Nilsen explains the current situation and gives details of his book: 'Even my lawyers have been denied access to four volumes of autobiography – which are not allowed to be sent outside of Home Office control and containment. These banned works amount to 4,000 typewritten pages of first-draft unedited script. Well, that's another story which will unfold through legal events in the fullness of time.'

When we recall the nature of his crimes, the reasons for the ban on his publication become clear. Between January 1978 and September 1981 he killed twelve men at his home in Melrose Avenue, London. One victim escaped: he had been taken back to the house, then had been to bed with Nilsen, and when the student woke the next day he felt very ill and had a severe headache. When he checked himself out he saw that he was bruised at the neck and his eyes were red. Nilsen had attempted to strangle him, but he was told that he had caught the flesh of his neck in a sleeping bag.

He had stated earlier on arrest that he was determined to have some company, even if that was with corpses. His first victim was buried under the floorboards, left there for several months, and then taken to the garden to be burned. He was found out when Dyno-Rod came to clear drains and human remains were discovered.

Even if his book analysed and responded to feelings about the killings, such topics are illegal for a prisoner to disseminate. After all, the works in print on him already offer plenty of bloody detail about the modus operandi of his murders. The murders in his home had filled up so much space in his efforts to hide the bodies that he had resorted to storing one victim under the kitchen sink. When DCI Jay arrived at the home, he reported that there was a noxious smell, and when asked to explain, Nilsen had said, with no sign of emotion that what the police searched for was in fact stored in various plastic bags. The items later found included two severed heads.

There have been psychological writings about Nilsen, and there has been a large volume of biography. As time has gone on, he himself has written on a range of subjects, as he is now writing for company. Inside the prison, he works in a Braille workshop, and there he has transcribed the texts of complete works into Braille for use in libraries in Africa. In fact, from the start, after his arrest, he has written. When he was arrested and the trial was approaching, he wrote copious notes and sketches, compiling fifty notebooks of his memories.

There was no diminished responsibility: his life inside since the trial has shown the perplexing aspect of duality which leads to a profile of a man who is generally referred to as 'sick and twisted' and a 'dangerous psychopath' but the person walking around the jail is quite the opposite: articulate, quiet and polite. It is almost as if there is a new identity occupying a shell. The dangerous occupant may still be down in the cellar, as it were, but the reasonable man answers the door.

It is hard to resist the speculation that the man now would essentially say the same as he did in 1984 when asked why he murdered those people. He was at Knightsbridge Crown Court, when appearing at the trial of Albert Moffat, who was charged with malicious wounding after attacking Nilsen in Wormwood Scrubs. He had slashed Nilsen's face with a razor, and the result was hospital attention amounting to eighty-nine stitches. Nilsen said, 'By nature I am not a violent person. You can look at my school reports, army and police service and nine years in the Civil Service and you'll find not one record of violence against me.'

His retort about the motive was 'Yes, it is a great enigma. These things were out of character. I killed people over a period of five years and it got worse.' He also told the court that in jail he never gloried in his publicity, and he said that he had not attacked Moffat, adding, 'Since I have been in prison I have felt no irresistible urge to kill someone.'

That makes sense: he had plenty of company. Some men spend hours in the prison library, poring over the stout and heavy books on criminal law, looking for loopholes and desperately searching for a line to thought that will open up the past to scrutiny. Dennis Nilsen wants his book to see the bookshop shelves, and he wants for people to listen, not to fall asleep. 'Then it will be okay.'

CHAPTER 14

Ian Brady:
Keeping Shtum

Before telling the story of Ian Brady in jail, I have my own experience on the Moors murders, something that happened to me quite by chance one day as I took some books out of my local library. It was the first time I had listened to a tale about Brady and Hindley from someone's mouth, rather than from the pages of a book.

At the issuing desk was Sandra, and we both started to chat about our interest in crime writing. I went to interview her after she said that she had been present during the investigations into those murders, based in Hyde.

Sandra has a good stock of scrapbooks about her involvement in one of the major murder enquiries in the history of crime. As we looked through them and she pointed out locations on the Saddleworth moors, or talked about a woman detective she knew, I felt as if I was revisiting a dark place in history. She showed me her photograph, as in the *Daily Mirror* at the time when Brady and Hindley were tried at Chester Assizes. Here was a woman with a story to tell, and it had been a long time since she showed these cuttings to anyone.

We met by chance. I write about true crime and spend hours in libraries and archives. Most of this work is about old newsprint and fading photos you find on a blurry microfilm image. But here was that rare thing, a chance to talk about a period in modern history when police work was just emerging from its *Blue Lamp* image and was being given to us as something close to the 'new documentary'. Not that it was being glamorised in the writing of the 1960s. Quiet heroism and career problems seemed to be the order of the day, and a PC was very non-PC by today's standards.

Sandra stepped into this world of mean streets and macho talk, and her photos show her wearing the stylish dark cape designed by no less a fashion guru than Norman Hartnall. But the impression she gives is that it wasn't macho at all – more gentlemanly. After all, this is the time in which it was considered unacceptable to swear on the football terraces if a woman was present. At the time, she was just taking up duties in Birkenhead. Her days as a secretary to the team of detectives who combed the wilds of Saddleworth were behind her. The Sandra of these images is every inch the professional, standing by a Panda car, or looking firm and controlled outside a police station. She displays the virtues of the British police as I recall them, in my teenage life in Leeds in the sixties: strong, visible, reliable, demanding respect.

The training course for this new life was at Padgate, Warrington. Sandra remembers this with real affection. 'It was the best time of my life ... I wept buckets when we had to leave', she says. Sandra knows the date as soon as she is asked: 6 October 1968. It was a year of riot and unrest over the Channel, and here we were losing several layers of innocence about modernity as well. You might say that at this point, our conceptions of the police were changing radically, as was the case with the entire notion of authority.

She notes that there was much pride in the training. There may have been a lively social side to the time, with entertainment being produced as part of the deal, but it was also tough. The drilling square was in use by eight in the morning and then it was down to some hard studying. All the details are still there as she fills in the picture. The famous cape was excellent quality, and the Cheshire force had a much better standard of dress than the Manchester outfit. Sandra tells me that some of the badges were enamelled. All the official photos show a woman completely comfortable in her position, status and very obvious responsibility. The car shines, well cared for. The hat and jacket are immaculate.

From the seminar room and the role plays it was out into the stuff of life. Her photographs reflect that quasi-military life and the facial expressions are firm, in control. Yes, she had experienced a certain notoriety during the previous few years, as fate brought her a central role in a media show as the tabloids struggled to find ways of extracting daily stories from Hyde while the force was out combing the moors. But nothing in that phase prepared Sandra for the police work on the streets. She had been only nineteen when she began work as secretary for Bob Talbot and the Moors team.

But in police work, she witnessed things that affected her deeply, such as being there when a mother callously rejected her own child, telling her to her face that she wanted nothing to do with her. 'That was the worst thing I ever saw' she says. But when I ask about the traumatic experiences in a police career, she smiles and says, 'We didn't do trauma ... there was no time.'

Whereas in the Moors investigation, she had sat in the incident room and answered the phone, now in uniform, she saw pain and suffering at first hand. She brings to mind one quiet Sunday morning and the harrowing experience of seeing the charred bodies of six children in the back of a car after a man had shot through some lights at high speed, just shattering the peace of that weekend lull in between the Saturday drunks and the afternoon in the park

Of course, I have to mention the image of the macho, unreformed male in the police, slotted into our conscious-ness through a thousand television dramas since *Z Cars*. But Sandra is eager to put me right on this one. She uses the word camaraderie, and explains that there was professional respect, and that teamwork was at the core of everything. She talks about 'gentlemanly' officers and a very different basis of relationships in the force, reflecting a world with just as many social problems as now, but maybe more easily understood and remedied.

As for her work in the Moors case, it is a fascinating chapter of history in the annals of modern police work. It was a steady, regular and ordered enquiry, with meticulous monitoring and recording. I picture her alone in the central office as the world's press darted around frantically outside. In a pre-computer age, the office work functioned around phone calls, record cards and a coded range of knocks on the office wall: one for tea, two for a useful communication and three for 'get out there now!'

The days of the enquiry were long and hard, Sandra being collected at eight thirty in the morning, taken to the office in

Hyde, and then work progressing steadily right through to eight at night.

The journalists and writers flocked to Hyde and to Sandra's office. She met Emlyn Williams, the author of the first book on the case, *Beyond Belief*. She and a friend were dogged by reporters and they sometimes had to hide. The whole business became so farcical that one day a newspaperman came into her office pretending to be ill. His performance was worthy of Olivier, but transparently sham. She had to fuss and seem concerned, while all the time watching him like a hawk.

The team managed to snatch an hour at the *Queen's Head* in Hyde for some bonding, but Sandra stresses that the talk on these occasions was strictly unwinding, easy small talk. There is nothing sensational in her memories of the time. It was 'just careful, routine work, as with any case . . . we had no idea at the time that this was to be momentous, and in so many books'.

She always wanted to be a police officer, from the time of her first job as a clerk in a magistrate's court, but never dreamed that a few years on from that, she would be snapped by the *Mirror* cameraman. I sense that, even today, when her early career and the story of those awful child-murders is 'classic crime' history, there is a certain respectful reserve in her attitude, and every sentence she utters has a tone of a less hectic time and a more people-centred time. I can imagine her on the beat or taking a call, and I feel assured that she would have been totally professional. Her most frequent word when talking about colleagues from that time is 'gentleman'.

After the interview, I understand why she chooses to say more about policing Birkenhead than what Myra Hindley said to her in the office. It has something to do with actually doing something positive to help out on the streets and in the unhappy homes. The psychopaths can be left to specialists and therapists, but there are plain folk out there being robbed and attacked or just drinking too much and disturbing the peace, and you can do something about that.

As she had sat in that office, at times there had been Ian Brady in the room behind her. Now he is an old man in jail and he has known no other life for decades.

The facts of his killings which took him to the prison cell are very well known. As Brady and Myra Hindley worked together and realised that they both had a relish for sadism; Brady was interested in Nazi ideologies as well, and when the couple went to live with Hindley's grandmother in Hattersley, Lancashire, Brady began to enjoy showing off his twisted imagination and love of weaponry to Hindley's young brother-in-law, David Smith. Crimes were talked about; but the talk became reality one day when Brady brought home a teenager called Edward Evans. Hindley went to fetch Smith and when he arrived at Brady and Hindley's place he watched Evans being murdered with an axe.

Smith called the police and the body was found and the search for the killers began. Suitcases were discovered in a left luggage store and there were weapons, tape recordings and other papers in a case. Tapes and other materials made it clear that two missing children, Lesley Ann Downey and John Kilbride, had been killed. Photos of the two killers out on Saddleworth Moors led police to the burial places, and the couple were arrested and tried at Chester Crown Court, being convicted in May 1966 and sentenced to life imprisonment.

The number of their victims has increased. A third grave was found in 1987 and the body of another victim, Keith Bennett, is almost certainly out on Saddleworth, but has not been found. From 1985, Brady and Hindley were involved in the desperate search for bodies, the two being taken out their to assist in the search.

Myra Hindley died in 2002, aged sixty, and had never been released, but Brady was declared criminally insane as early as 1985. The explanations for their heinous acts have been many and varied. But there's one consensus: that a violent psychopath met a woman who also lived in a violent world, and the result was a horrific killing spree.

Brady's prison life has always made the headlines. In October 1999 he had been staging a long hunger strike and after thirty days was force-fed. At that time he was sixty-one and had refused food for a month as he was protesting about being moved to another ward in Ashworth secure hospital in Merseyside. The story was that he had been forcibly moved to the top security Lawrence Ward and that he was supposed to have broken a wrist in that transfer. But what is to be believed is always a tough question in the Brady saga. He wanted, and still wants, to die. But Ashworth authorities felt that they had to intervene as they were bound by a duty of care. The Prison Service is also bound by that duty, and will not generally intervene. Officers will endure a long and tiring suicide 'bed watch' in cases of high risk, but in Brady's instance, to die is his will. Brady's lawyer in 1999 tried to have a court injunction issued to prevent intervention. The lawyer told *The Independent*, 'The critical issue is this: do the authorities have the right to force-feed somebody who does not want to be force-fed – even if that means they may die?'

In his ward, a knife had been found taped under a sink, and so security was tightened. That move to the ward and the security move, prompted Brady's strike. The incident was a key event in Brady's long saga of complaints of abuse and rough handling inside; he wrote letters claiming that he had been assaulted and that his arms had been so severely injured by officers that he had not been able to write for ten days.

The moans go on. In 2008, he said, 'I am the sole high-profile prisoner Ashworth holds to exploit as a demonizing agent.' He expressed concern that his wages were low and that he was maltreated. This long letter was to his MP, George Howarth and also to his solicitor. The drift of his main argument was that civil liberties in general are being eroded, but more particularly, he stated there that his prison wages of £25 a week were unfair, as most prisoners he said, earn £100. The fact is that payments in wages inside depend on what the person actually does to earn cash.

He aimed at fellow prisoners in the letter as well: 'Perhaps more embarrassing to prudently financial New Labour are the ranks of tramps and malingerers who have escaped into Ashworth to avoid working for a living, demanding and receiving full board and benefits ...' He turns attention to himself, noting that his cataracts had been untreated for ten years because he would not be taken to a hospital as his 'visiting an outside hospital would attract unwanted attention'.

In 2008, his solicitor told the press: 'The change in the therapeutic environment at Ashworth since the late 1990s has led Mr Brady to wish to be transferred back to prison. He wishes to be free from the power of psychiatrists under the Mental

Health Act, including the power to artificially prolong his life by force feeding.'

Brady is now the longest serving prisoner in England and Wales. He has explained his hunger strike, which still goes on, by referring to Myra: 'Myra gets the potentially fatal brain condition, whilst I have to fight simply to die. I have had enough. I want nothing, my objective is to die and release myself from this once and for all. So you see my death strike is rational and pragmatic.'

His prison career has been peppered with incident and sensation. As far back as 1970, while he was in the top security E Wing at HMP Durham the papers reported an attack on him. The standard prison attack of throwing hot sugared tea into someone's face was done by Brady on another prisoner called Morris. Sugar is regarded as a risk on the prison wings. Sugar in tea makes the hot liquid stick and burn more intensely. In 1970, Raymond Morris attacked Brady in retaliation and both were then confined to their cells for twenty-eight days.

In 1971, the issue of where to keep Brady was up for debate. The Home Secretary then was Reginald Maudling, and he was pressured into making a decision on this. It is amazing to note that at the time, the Durham E Wing was used to house just two men: Brady and John Straffen, the child killer. *The Times* reported that the wing 'could more usefully be used to house up to 400 prisoners'. Maudling wanted to transfer Brady to Broadmoor but the Department of Health were opposed to that move. The whole situation caused the E Wing at Durham to be held in limbo, as it was due for closure, and that was suspended until a decision on Brady was reached.

When he eventually went to Broadmoor, the hunger strikes began and the subject went as far as parliament. Roy Jenkins told the House that the doctor responsible for Brady had made the decision, but another MP said that 'Most of us thought . . . that the practice of artificial feeding in response to hunger strikes was ended.' There was a feeling in the air that most would want Brady dead. The MP for Berwick said, 'Most of us . . . feel that it is implicit that neither he nor the prison authorities have any obligation to seek to prolong the life of a person like Brady against his determined wishes . . .'

The years passed and every move Brady seemed to make caused a stir up to the more recent plateau in which an impasse has been reached. In 1978, a letter he wrote managed to find its way into a national paper. He was at the time a category A prisoner in Wormwood Scrubs. The explanation given to parliament was that 'Inquiries at the prison suggest that the letter was one sent to an acquaintance in the normal way. A letter which was recognized as intended for publication would be stopped, but such an intention may not always be apparent.'

By 1980, with the support of Lord Longford who had been in touch with Brady, the debate as to where to move Brady for a more permanent residence was hot again, and Longford announced that doctors who had treated Brady at Broadmoor and at Gartree agreed that he should be taken to Park Lane, Liverpool. That happened in November 1985 when *The Times* announced that he was in Park Lane, but added: 'If Brady's mental health improves sufficiently he can expect to be sent back to prison to continue serving his sentence.' But the Home Office had said at the time that there was not to be any consideration about his parole and could not happen until another ten years had passed.

Writing this in 2010, I am aware that Brady still lingers in that no-man's land which is a kind of antechamber to death. He wants to go through that door to oblivion. He has been a notorious prisoner for so long that his infamy rests now on a repulsive image of an old man waiting for death, and he has been in that state for a very long time.

He had been a guest of Her Majesty long before his sentence for murder. He was sent to a Borstal in 1955, coming back out into society in November 1957. He had always found mountains and moors to be in some way imaginatively arousing. One psychiatrist told Duncan Staff, who wrote *The Lost Boy,* a book about the Moors murders, that on a trip out of Glasgow when a boy, and living with his adoptive parents, he had 'fallen into a trance' at the sight of mountains. He added that for him they had a 'pantheistic, almost religious significance'.

Ian Brady lies there now, in his bed at Ashworth, surely dreaming of mountains and keeping his secrets. As a notorious prisoner, he has both bored us and intrigued us, and truths will be buried with him, whether we like it or not.

CHAPTER 15

Jeremy Bamber:
Endless Campaign

The first time I ever worked as a writer in a prison, it was in Full Sutton, and there I gave, with another writer, a talk on poetry. My first book had just been published and I recall that I read a few poems in that classroom in the education department, having no idea who was in the room. There were around thirty men there, and they listened intently and then asked questions at the end. One of them showed me their writing magazine: it was one of the best I had ever seen, and in my life as a writer in residence I have produced many magazines. In the group at the time was Jeremy Bamber, and I feel sure he got something out of the session. He comes across to the media as articulate, expressive and creative. Many people behind bars are like that, but he has made a point of telling the world that he is so, and he appears to believe that opinions of him will change, and that perhaps one day people will listen to his 'truths' of what happened on the day of the White House Farm murders in 1985.

In August 1985, the bodies of Nevill Bamber, June Bamber, Sheila Caffell and her two children Daniel and Nicholas, were found gunned to death in the Nevill farmhouse at White House Farm, near Tolleshunt D'Arcy in Essex. The police had been rung by Jeremy Bamber, adopted son of the family, expressing the fear that his sister Sheila was mentally insane and was about to go crazy with a gun. On the way to the farm the police passed a Citreon which was moving slowly; Bamber was in the car, aiming to arrive after the police on the death scene.

From those two facts – the phone call and the slow car – matters were to change and the focus was placed on Bamber as a suspect, after the initial police belief that the scene was indeed indicative of Sheila slaughtering the family and then taking her own life. She had a history of mental illness and the local community were aware of her strange outbursts from time to time. The turning point in the enquiry was when Bamber's girlfriend, Julie Mugford, talked to the police about Bamber and his plan to kill the family to obtain the inheritance.

Jeremy Bamber had been adopted by this wealthy farming family. June was a very religious person and tended to force her beliefs on her adopted children (Sheila was also adopted and worked to a limited extent as a model). Jeremy was sent away to have an expensive education, even going to the famous Gresham's School in Norfolk, and then later he gained some GCEs nearer home. The plan was for him to learn to be a businessman and estate manager. He had his own house and an income. Nevill clearly wanted his son to work and learn, rather than wait and inherit without a foundation knowledge required for the squire's life.

Nevill did lead the life of a squire: hunting with his dog, shooting rabbits, living in a place with a massive acreage and a fine house at the centre. But Jeremy did not want to work and wait. Julie Mugford told the Essex police that Jeremy had spent a long time planning the murders; she explained that he hated his mother, and usually called her 'an old cow'. He detested the life with his adopted parents but would not leave them. Julie told the police that he stayed because he had said, ' I have too much to lose. It's important to have money when you're young.'

The day before the deaths, he had rung Julie and said that it had to happen that night or it never would. She never warned the Bambers, almost certainly believing that Jeremy was drunk and had no real intention of actually killing the family. But he loved guns and he had not only been brought up amongst shooting pieces; at school he was in a place which was famous for its army cadet force. He was a good shot. Julie had struggled to hold in what she knew after learning that there really had been a mass murder. The police, after listening to her, thought again about what had been defined as a clear-cut case of slaughter by a mad woman who had shot herself through the head after killing her own children and adopted parents.

Time has passed and the blame for the wrong-headed thinking about the crime scene has been placed on DI Ronald Cook and his team, who allegedly made mistakes in the hours after arriving at the scene. The evidence had suggested to these officers that the crime was an extreme example of a 'domestic'. In terms of Sheila's wounds, Dr Craig, the police surgeon, saw that there were two wounds on her: one shot had gone through her jugular vein and the other had gone through the chin and up into the brain. If this was suicide, then the first shot had to be into the vein, giving her some seconds to fire again and die very quickly as the brain was smashed.

But after Julie's words to the police, there was fresh thinking and that has gone on to this day, with a number of new findings emerging over 2009 and early 2010 in particular. The first line of thought was about the necessary struggle involved: Nevill was a tall man, and still strong at sixty-one. The killer would have had to fight him. Yet there were no bruises or marks of a struggle on Sheila. Soon after, it was realized that the practical aspect of Sheila lying down and raising a rifle with a silencer on above her, so she could fire through her chin, was of great value. In effect, the gun would have been too long for her to handle in that way.

While this was going on, Jeremy Bamber was away on holiday in St Tropez with his New Zealander friend, Brett Collins. When Bamber arrived back at Dover, he was arrested and charged with murder. At the trial Bamber stood firm against questioning. Anthony Arlidge fired questions at him which went to the heart of the matter:

Arlidge:	You did shoot the first four people with that silencer didn't you?
Bamber:	That is not true.
Arlidge:	Then you shot Sheila with the silencer on?
Bamber:	That is untrue.
Arlidge:	When you came to fake her suicide, you realized it was not possible for her to shoot herself with the silencer on?
Bamber:	That is untrue.

What had happened in further enquiries was that a silencer was found in a cupboard, smeared with blood. The first police

officers on the scene had failed to find this. But after the discovery, a more meaningful narrative of the murderous events
was put together.

The jury took some considerable time to reach a decision.
In the end a majority verdict was accepted by the judge, Mr
Justice Drake and with a vote of 10–2 the verdict was guilty.
Bamber was sentenced to life imprisonment with a ruling that
at least twenty-five years had to be served before parole could
be considered. The sentence was one of five concurrent life
sentences. It was noted that Bamber opened the door of the
dock himself. But his exit from the court was just the beginning
of a lengthy saga of arguments, appeals and legal preoccupations
from Bamber, one of the most litigious and vociferous prisoners
in the establishment. For decades he has campaigned, insisting
on his innocence. The general public probably have an image of
him fixed in their minds, weeping at the family funeral; he was
also a very handsome and attractive young man. Women were
drawn to him and he had charm.

The ongoing campaign for a case review has included
several gambits from the cell at Full Sutton. He recently took
a lie detector test and although the results of a polygraph are
not admissible in Britain, the lawyer for Bamber wrote to the
Home Secretary to ask for his client's release. After two refused
applications for appeals in 1987 and 2002, we might have felt
that everything had come to and end and that acceptance was
in order. Not one bit was this the case.

Jeremy Bamber is the quintessential example of the prisoner
who constantly takes on the system. This type studies the law
books, discusses legislation and argues every step taken by the
Prison Service. A prison regime involves an almost infinite
number of security measures; daily routine is built around following prison regulations and correct procedure. A modern prison
has to do things by the book, meticulously and thoroughly. Gone
are the days when, as with the story of Harry Roberts, large
tools may be smuggled inside or holes made in cell walls. There
are regular and often unannounced spins, cell searches, under-
taken to look for such illegal items as mobile phones or even
makeshift weapons.

In April 2009, Bamber wrote to *Inside Time* newspaper that
he had 'lost a landmark case'. He wrote: 'My complaint was

that officers are now searching the cell rather than simply doing bars and bolts. During an official search, our legal documents are put into a bag in front of us and sealed.' He then alleged that copies of legal material had been given to police liaison officers by prison security staff. If true, then he has a valid and important point to make. Otherwise, with him it has become a classic example of 'the boy who cried wolf' because he has had so many complaints and objections to prison discipline.

From the first stint he did inside at Wormwood Scrubs, he has attracted notice, and that is exactly and primarily what he wants. The writer and poet, Ken Smith, worked as writer in residence at the Scrubs at the time and he noted that Bamber was 'Under close supervision all the time. He was not popular on the wing.' I have listened to accounts from former wing-mates of his alleging that Bamber was so much in fear of attack that he was in the habit of wrapping thick copies of *Country Life* magazine around him to protect him from knife attacks. That may or may not be true, but the story goes around the prison population, which has an oral history of its own, separate from anything in print.

Bamber also attracted attention in the first phase of his life inside from young women. He was visited by Anji Greaves for a while – a very attractive woman who worked as a beautician – and he told her how much she exuded sex appeal. That was while he was in his long remand period: after the sentence, the relationship ended. Other women visited as well. One woman told the press, 'I can't believe he's the evil monster he's made out to be. He said he's innocent and I believe him.'

Even after just one month following his conviction, an appeal was launched; the argument was that the judge had been biased in his summing-up, stressing that Sheila Caffell had not been capable of the attack on her adopted father. Then, in 1988, Bamber must have realised how far he had fallen into oblivion because he was taken out of jail to a tribunal to try to have some ownership of the land and estate at the Bamber's home. This failed and of course, as he had a murder conviction, the inheritance is never going to happen.

This long series of events relating to the crime and to prison life would still continue to be no more than irksome and irritating to the authorities. A full-length book by Scott Lomax has detailed alleged shortcomings in police communications in relation to the murders, but this is nothing compared to the development which has occurred in February 2010. In a letter to the press it has been revealed that Peter Smethurst, a forensic specialist, has reported that there is an anomaly in the photographic evidence at the scene of the crime. The *Express* summarized: 'It was claimed that Bamber was in a violent struggle with 61-year-old Nevill in the kitchen of their home … in the early hours of August 7, 1985. During the struggle the end of the silencer caused scratch marks on the underside of a shelf above the Aga cooker. Now expert Peter Smethurst says photos taken hours after the murder do not show scratch marks. He concludes that the marks were made a month after the crime …'

This report has gone to the Criminal Cases Review Commission and they have had the photo in question enlarged. Bamber claims that 'further examination of the floor area in the kitchen shows that there is absolutely no paint debris of any sort from approximately 60 cm of scratch marks that penetrate up to eleven layers of paint in places'. How he would know about the layers of paint is open to question, but the fact is that someone has stepped in now, into this chink of light in the reappraisals done by forensic science, and that man is Herbert Leon MacDonell.

MacDonell has been a leading forensic expert for forty years; his speciality is in blood-spatter analysis, and he has been involved in a number of prominent cases over the years. In 1960, he invented the MAGNA Brush fingerprint device which changed the process of fingerprint evidence . It has no bristles and so it made it possible to avoid the problem of a ridge being formed as a print was tested and recorded. Then, in 1971, he wrote *Flight Characteristics and Stain Patterns of Human Blood* which was officially endorsed by the US Department of Justice. This is basically a guide to blood-spatter analysis for police personnel. MacDonell later became the director of the Laboratory of Forensic Science in Corning, New York. His status as a consultant is so revered that he has been engaged to participate in cases such as the OJ Simpson trial and even in the investigations conducted into the assassination of Robert Kennedy.

His standard work which explains his major cases is *The Evidence Never Lies: The Casebook of a Modern Sherlock Holmes.*

'Sherlock' MacDonell has looked at the images of the photos in question. The issue is really whether or not the body of Sheila Caffell was moved by police. MacDonell has said that in his view, the photos show that there was an unexplained 'movement' of the body during the time that a whole set of pictures were taken by police. *The Guardian* reported on 15 March 2009, 'The newly disclosed images suggest the rifle used in the killings was at some point moved from her body, strengthening the suggestion she was murdered instead of committing suicide.'

In 2008, at the last appeal, Bamber was told by the judge, Mr Justice Tugendhat, that he would spend the rest of his life behind bars for such an exceptionally serious crime. That is now looking to be a less likely forecast. Bamber's solicitors, Chivers of Bingley, are reported to have obtained copies of the Essex Police notes taken from that fateful morning at White House Farm, and they have stated that there was a 'movement' inside the house at the time Bamber was outside the property and was in fact with the police.

The case may emerge as one in which fundamental errors were made at the first stage of forensic work and, as Vernon Geberth, the Commander of Bronx Homicide NYDD told writer Connie Fletcher in her book, *Real Crime Scene Investigations*, 'Do it right the first time. You only get one chance. Once things have been moved, once things have been changed, once you lose that little window of opportunity, it's gone forever.'

The White House Farm case is fast accruing a vast library of data: opinions, reports, appeals, letters and photographs. There has even been talk of the place having some kind of hex on it, because the previous owner, Frank Page, was found drowned in a horse-trough, and the owner before Page hanged himself inside the house. The literature around the case goes on being written. Bamber had a website and many people will have grazed there; the book by Scott Lomax has made some readers think again. The heart of the matter may well turn out to be the actions (or lack of actions) taken by Cook when the first scene of crime measures were taken. But although questions remain, there is a feeling in the air that the saga has one last act yet to be performed.

CHAPTER 16

John Straffen: Fifty-five Years Inside

Prison officers have not written many books about their lives. Maybe very few in their ranks have any urge to write down experiences; after all, who would want to take that line of work home with them and make books out of their lives? One person who has, thankfully, done so, is Robert Douglas. Not only has he given readers one of the very rare examples of a man being detailed to work with a condemned man back in the days of capital punishment; he has also left a memory of being on the Durham E Wing when John Straffen was there. As he looked out into the exercise area, Douglas saw a man who was a very striking figure. He wrote: 'A tall, solitary prisoner is exercising ... striding out. He wears a blue cotton jacket, buttoned up under his chin. His head is shaved. All he needs are a couple of bolts through his neck and he'd be a dead ringer for Frankenstein.'

The man watched the wire and when two birds landed on it, he shook the wire to chase them away. He was amused by doing that, Douglas noticed, and adds, 'I look at him as he passes by. He exudes strangeness, menace.' He asked the other officers if the man was out for a punishment, and anyway who was he? When Douglas was told it was John Straffen his response was, 'Straffen! Bloody hell! This is a name from my childhood. I would've thought this reptile would have died years ago ... As I grew up, began to try and read the papers and saw news-reels, now and again there would be some big murder case ...' Thousands of people would agree with that. The name Straffen had become a word that was known through the tabloids and the broadcasts, a name to cause a shiver of revulsion.

If writing is largely about trying to apply some empathy to the subject and to imagine what another life would be like, then to contemplate what Straffen's mind must have been in fifty-five years of incarceration is surely beyond any writer's ability. When he was found guilty of the murder of a girl, Linda Bowyer, in July 1952, he was initially sentenced to death, but that was reduced to life inside. He had already killed two young girls for which he had been tried at Somerset assizes in 1951. Straffen had been declared a 'mental defective' in 1947 and had been sent to an asylum. After being found unfit to stand trial for the first killings he was sent to Broadmoor.

In this way the massive stretch of fifty-five years began. In his first location, Broadmoor, he managed to escape, and he went out to kill again. The Broadmoor alarm system is sounded every Monday morning at ten in the morning, as a practice run for a real escape alarm. But when Straffen escaped, there were no sirens. He was free to stroll into the nearest village and take a life.

In 1952, Straffen was doing cleaning routines when he found a way out; he clambered onto the roof of a hut and climbed to freedom, then he walked to the nearest village at Arborfield and there he met five-year-old Linda and strangled her. His murderous tendencies were something that just a little earlier in history would have labelled him 'criminally insane' and that term certainly held good for his nature when he struck again after his escape.

Straffen's first murder happened when he came across little Brenda Goddard at Rough Hill, in Bath, where Straffen was born. He was just twenty-one and was compelled to go to children, place his hands on their necks and strangle them to death, as he did with Brenda. Only a few days after that he came across Cicely Batstone, who was a little older; they met at the cinema and he walked out with her; and he strangled her in a field. He was woken up by police and had no idea what he had done, or so he said. But his confession soon followed.

When he died in November 2007, he was Britain's longest-serving prisoner and the press made the most of it. He died in the health care unit at HMP Frankland.

In prison, a person finds strategies of survival if he has a sense of reality and a perception of himself as a person within a known community, but if he has, as Shakespeare said of King Lear 'Ever but slenderly known himself' then the experience of life inside will be a timeless frame of routine experience in which the fantasy or the dark imagination wallowing inside will fill the vacuum. Robert Douglas saw a shell of a man, and yet he was enjoying disturbing the little birds. Something in him wanted to destroy what was pure, defenceless and innocent, much as small boys swat flies or stand on insects.

But even with this in mind, the fact is that we are still talking about horrendous murders in the Straffen story. His tale begins with him being taken to a Child Guidance Clinic for truancy and petty theft, in 1938; then he was in court for the first time and given probation. It became clear to professionals that he had no moral sense, and he was analysed by a psychiatrist. That is when the term 'mental defective' was applied to him. But he was still at school up to the age of sixteen and at that time, he was assessed as having an IQ of just 64. He tried to do normal work back home in Bath but he was an isolated figure, stealing from houses and being alienated from human society.

In July 1947, he was arrested. A girl had been attacked and the assailant had grabbed her, saying, 'What would you do if I killed you? I have done it before.' It was clear that he could not be allowed to live in society and so he was sent to what was then called a 'colony'. In the fifties, I can recall the shiver of fear that passed through myself and family or friends when a certain phrase was spoken: 'They'll send you to an *institution*' That word, coined in the Victorian period, has a resonance through the British psyche. Children who were 'strange' or 'retarded' – the words used at the time – could be taken away and never come out to play or sit in school again. Such was the fate of John Straffen.

But when he was a little older and back in Bath, he did the first murder. The Batstone murder took place in an area known as 'Tumps' and in the day's walking around cinemas and streets with the girl, he had been seen by many people. Straffen and Cicely had even been seen by a policeman's wife. He was soon found. After a hearing at Bath Magistrates' Court he was committed for trial at Taunton assizes, appearing on 17 October 1951.

At court in Bath, all Straffen could say to account for what he had done with Cicely was, 'She was picking flowers and I told her there would be plenty higher up. I lifted her over the wall. She never screamed even when I squeezed her neck, so I bashed her head against the wall.' But there had been further explanation of exactly what had happened when he had spoken to a police officer. *The Times* reported this:

> He carried out a demonstration in which he held Sergeant Evans facing outwards against his left breast, put his hands around his neck and squeezed. Later, Straffen said, 'She had her back to me when I squeezed her neck. She went limp. I did not feel sorry. I forgot about it. I went back over the wall. I had no feeling about it. I forgot about it.'

Then, at Taunton, Straffen was found unfit to plead. He was ordered to be detained at Her Majesty's Pleasure, and so an explanation was needed, and Dr Peter Parkes, medical officer at HMP Horsfield, said that Straffen had been in custody as a mental defective and had been released on licence. He described Straffen as feeble minded, and Mr Justice Oliver told the court: 'You might as well try a baby in arms. If a man cannot understand what is going on he cannot be tried.'

His destination was Broadmoor, and so he made the escape. That was to be the start of a furore about security at that special secure hospital. After the body of Linda Bowyer had been found, Straffen was found at Crowthorne and arrested. He said simply, 'I did not kill her. That's a frame-up that is.' He was sent on remand to Brixton prison, but there followed a massive protest when it became widely reported that he had escaped from Broadmoor, to kill again. In early May 1952 there was a protest meeting at Crowthorne, presided over by the chairman of the parish council and the MP was there too. A resolution was passed in which the parishioners expressed 'horror and alarm' at the escape. They asked for a system of public warning to be put in place and that there should be such a discipline in place in Broadmoor that escapes would be impossible. They also wanted the Home Office to be put in control of the institution.

Members of that council went to Broadmoor specifically to be informed about the circumstances which had led to Straffen's escape. Two months later a report on Boadmoor was produced for the government by the Ministry of Health; a siren warning was planned, and also there was to be 'a prearranged plan of cooperation between the staff of the institution and the police'. It was stated that there had been a failure to exercise close supervision of inmates and some facts were given in the report: 'The present staff is 19 below complement, and there appears little likelihood of sufficient staff being recruited in the near future.' The first siren plan was described also: 'There should be a distinctive siren or other audible warning to be operated by the responsible officer on duty at Broadmoor as soon as an escape has been detected. This should be coupled electrically to an alarm in Wokingham police station.'

The formative moment in John Straffen's life, the beginning of his decades in jail, was at Winchester Assizes when he was tried for the murder done after his escape. This was a Court of Criminal Appeal; the grounds for this were put by Henry Elam, as stated in the press:

> That Mr Justice Cassels was wrong at the trial in admitting evidence of two other murders of little girls alleged to have been committed by Straffen at Bath on July 15 and August 8, 1951.
>
> That he was also wrong in admitting evidence of an oral statement made to two detective inspectors on April 30 when the appellant was in custody without the usual warning first being administered to him.

This smacks of desperation and indeed the appeal was quashed. Mr Justice Slade said that the general rule was to exclude evidence which tended to show that the accused had been guilty of criminal acts other than those covered by the indictment. The similarities between the Bath and Crowthorne cases were considered and a decision made. The judges said that the evidence was properly admitted and dismissed the appeal.

There followed Straffen's long prison life, and as the years rolled by, there were occasional reports of him being moved, as in 1966 when he was transferred from Horfield prison in Bristol to Parkhurst on the Isle of Wight, where there was a new security wing. There had been an escape attempt by a group of prisoners at Wandsworth and they had wanted to take Straffen with them. The locals wanted him moved and he went to Cardiff at first and then later to Horfield.

He went to Parkhurst, followed shortly by six of the Great Train Robbers. That was in 1966, just before he was moved yet again, to Durham, where Robert Douglas met him. Successive Home Secretaries consistently refused to free Straffen and in 1994 a special list was compiled of life-term prisoners who must never see the outside world again: Straffen was on that list. In 2002, his application to be considered by the Criminal Cases Review Commission was refused.

We are left with a recurring problem about insanity and the law. What does society do with such people – the ones who are always going to be dangerous to the public? Some will be occupied in education and forms of self-development. They may be quite capable of study and conversation, and of genuine learning processes. Yet there are others, like Straffen, who are destined to be locked in and observed, constantly supervised and checked. They live in a static condition, isolated and shut into their dark imaginations. For some, his death was merely a desirable cut in the expenses of keeping such a dangerous man away from his prey; while for others it was another reminder that we are powerless to affect, change or cure the sick minds of those beyond therapy and outside workable understanding.

CHAPTER 17

Sutcliffe:
Every Day a Torment

I am beginning with a story that forms a fragment of my own autobiography, and it is something that throws light on how the years of the Ripper's regime in West Yorkshire impinged on virtually everyone around the Leeds and Bradford conurbation. Between 1975 and 1981 the effects of the serial killings he committed were like a seismic rumble of fear and apprehension across the county; women were thinking carefully before travelling anywhere alone and parents worked hard to take extra protective measures with their daughters. The Ripper years brought all kinds of stories, and the public did not know much of the background tales and the repulsive details of the modus operandi until later when the retrospective books and articles were written.

In my family photograph album there is a picture of Churwell Working Men's Club football team, dated around 1950. My father is in the picture, and one of his team-mates was related to a Ripper victim. I recall seeing him play on the Tanhouse pitch just between Churwell and the Elland Road football ground and the post-war prefabs by the cemetery at Gelderd Road. This is only a footnote to the Ripper story, but it has touched me and mine, as it did so many Yorkshire people. As a teenager, I used to walk to a stamp shop next to the Gaiety cinema in Harehills. A decade after that time, Sutcliffe would be hunting for prey in streets by the cinema, and one of his victims there was the Churwell woman, sister to the footballer. I'm relating this to stress to readers who don't know the Ripper's hunting grounds that it is impossible to evade the repugnant essence of depravity that still hangs over local memories; it is almost as if the Leeds and Bradford streets, and their counterparts in

Huddersfield and Halifax, retain some traces of his evil, like ghosts linger in oppressed houses.

There is so much in print about the horrific and murderous acts of Peter Sutcliffe, the Yorkshire Ripper, that there is no need to retell everything in depth here, but before his prison life is traced, here are some summarising facts.

The career of the Yorkshire Ripper has the trajectory so often linked to that version of psychopath who has to begin with tentative approaches to possible victims, and gradually raise the risks and the excitement levels to the point at which a killing has to take place, and it has to be done in a certain way. In this case, one of the earliest attacks fortunately did not end in a death. This was in Keighley, early on the Saturday morning, 5 July, when Anna Rogulskyj was viciously attacked from behind. She had been cracked with a hammer three times and was amazingly still alive – but only just – and she was rushed to hospital. It was then found that she had also been cut across the stomach. It took a twelve-hour operation to save her life.

In 1974, it seems highly likely that there was a Ripper attack in Bradford, this one on Gloria Wood, who survived. Gloria was a student at the time and on 11 November, as she was walking across a school field, she met a man who seemed kind, she was laden down with heavy bags and he said he would help. But she says that he began to strike her with a claw-hammer. She only survived because there were people nearby who disturbed the ritual that the Ripper needed. Gloria's description of the assailant was that he was medium height, with a short curly beard and dark hair, wearing a dark suit. Her skull was fractured, and she was clearly very close to being on the list of murder victims.

There are other possible victims beginning to be recorded and discussed, mainly due to a television programme, broadcast in 1996, *Silent Victims: The Untold Story of the Yorkshire Ripper*. The documentary dealt with six attacks and most of these seem highly likely to be put down as Sutcliffe cases. Gloria Wood's attack was perhaps the most plain one to link to him, but there are other brief accounts, maybe all part of the sequence in that early phase, when he was gaining a twisted kind of confidence in his sick and brutal regime.

In August 1996, for instance, a housewife in Lister Hills was attacked in the early hours of the morning: she was stabbed in the stomach. Earlier, in 1992, according to Keith Hellawell in his book of memoirs, an Irish student was attacked in Bradford, as reported at the time. Yet the documentary attaches the crime to Leeds. The tendency is for crime historians to want to link any brutal murder committed around the Leeds-Bradford conurbation in these years to the Ripper. Even some murders which have no features of a Ripper attack have been suggested, such as the unsolved murder of Mary Judge near Leeds Parish Church in 1968, which is clearly not the work of Sutcliffe.

But in the facts around the murder of Tina Atkinson on 23 April 1977 there is no doubt about the identity of the killer. She was a divorced mother who worked as a prostitute, based in a flat, and she returned home one day to find the Ripper there, making all circumstances easy for him to strike. Tina had had a great deal to drink, and had enjoyed a pub crawl looking for business. When she left the *Carlisle* pub just after ten on a warm Saturday evening she was noticed. She carried on working for a while, then went to her flat.

The next day, early evening, one of her close friends went to check on her and to have a chat; he was to find her mutilated body on the bed. The pathologist on the scene, Dr Gee, was the first medical man to have to write up a report of what was to become a sickeningly familiar tale across Yorkshire: a chisel had been used, and she had been stabbed in the body and neck. She had not been raped. It is staggering to note just how much alcohol was in her body – twenty spirit measures – and we have to wonder how much she knew about anything that went on that night, particularly as she was struck as soon as she entered the room.

In January 1978, Yvonne Pearson's body was found under a dumped sofa in a waste site. This was perhaps the most disgustingly brutal attack, as she had been struck so violently and relentlessly on her skull that it had fragmented into twenty-one pieces. To do this nasty work of destruction, a heavy ball-hammer had been used. As a final humiliation, some old stuffing material from the sofa had been rammed into her gullet. This time, there was nothing to denote the usual stabbing, but the hammer and the sexual elements to the killing pointed to the Ripper. Ironically, Yvonne had been heard to say on one occasion, 'It would be just my luck to meet the Ripper.'

At this stage, the operation to catch the killer was being increased and more men deployed. In April 1979, the event happened that was to divert the investigations and arguably made the last killings more manageable for the Ripper: this was the arrival of the Wearside Jack tapes, sent to George Oldfield who led the investigation. Valuable time was spent in gathering experts and scholars to study the tape and to trace the location of the speaker, as he had a distinct Wearside accent. The focus shifted from West Yorkshire to Castletown near Sunderland. Though the general paranoia about the identity of the Ripper went on, there was less intense concentration on the Bradford conurbation. Forensic linguistic expert, Stanley Ellis of Leeds University did an amazing job of analyzing the voice on the tape, isolating the local accent of 'Jack'. How was he to know that the police would be convinced that the voice was Sutcliffe – and be wrong?

Now of course we know the identity of Wearside Jack and his venture into fantasy and a reign of terror that ensued can be blamed for the continued Ripper killings around Leeds when attention was diverted to Wearside. Before that, as oral history testimony makes clear, the Ripper tapes had been broadcast in every possible location. Thousands of people have recalled their feelings of terror on hearing that voice, clearly based on the infamous hoax letters written to the Metropolitan Police back in the days of the original Ripper in Whitechapel, in 1888.

During this period, the eleventh victim was found: student Barbara Leach had enjoyed a night out at the *Manville Arms* in Bradford, and after this she decided to walk home alone: just the thing that the police had been advising women not to do. She only managed to walk around twenty yards before he struck. Student flatmates assumed she was sleeping somewhere else, but they were worried the next day. Her body was found under an old carpet, in an alley. Bricks had been piled on this. The scene provided the usual degrading and seedy atmosphere, as he chose to haunt the back alleys and yards of the northern towns.

Barbara had even asked a flatmate to wait up for her. She had said that she just wanted a walk, after stepping out of the pub into Great Horton Road; it was a quarter to one. The search for her took a few days, and there was still a faint hope that she might turn up for an appointment that had been made for 12.30 on the next Monday. She never arrived and not long after, a constable found the body. It was a shocking experience for PC Simon Greaves.

It is instructive to look back at those years with the knowledge of hindsight, and to be aware of David Canter's concept of mapping in profile work. It all looks so simple now: thirteen murders and at least eleven attacks, all within a twenty mile radius of Bradford's centre (with the exception of the Manchester killing). It all points to a person living close to Bradford, taking the excursions to places he could reach within a set period of time, and from where he could return to his lair smoothly and quickly.

The file on other potential victims of the Sutcliffe campaign will inevitably go on. The documents linked to the Byford Report on the way the police dealt with the case had some spin-offs in this ongoing investigation, and the author of *Wicked Beyond Belief*, a full story of the Yorkshire Ripper, by Michael Bilton, makes use of these documents. This suggests that anything else likely to emerge now that might be related to these murders will be marginal and perhaps difficult to substantiate.

A summary of his known victims helps to define exactly what a relentless killer the man was. First came Wilma McCann on 30 October 1975 in Leeds; the police at the time thought she was a part-time prostitute and that her death had happened because she had unluckily come across one of those clients who turned nasty and perhaps did not want to pay for her services. She was killed only a short distance from her home, her body being dragged into some nearby playing fields.

The second victim was Emily Jackson from Churwell, near Morley. The Jacksons had the habit of going to the *Gaiety* pub on the fringe of Chapeltown, a Leeds red-light district, and Emily was allegedly out in search of sex on the night of 20 January 1976 when she did not return to her waiting husband in the pub. The next day her mutilated body was found in some derelict buildings. There was then a lull until the third victim, Irene Richardson, a prostitute, was found dead in a park on 6 February 1977. This was at Roundhay, where there had previously been an attack, on Marcella Claxton, and she had survived.

The fourth was Tina Atkinson in Bradford, and she met her clients in her flat, where her body was found. She had taken Sutcliffe back there one night, 23 April 1977. DCS Domaille went to the crime scene. What he found was described by Michael Bilton in one of the most comprehensive Ripper books: 'The woman had probably bled to death on the bed. Her dark hair was soaked in blood, as were the sheets and pillow ... Her arms were spread out down her side ... Her white cotton pants had been pulled down to expose her buttocks ...' But what Domaille noticed most acutely was a large bloodstain on a wooden chair; then he saw a bloodstained leather jacket in the wardrobe. A narrative of events was built up. One might have thought at the time that the police were getting closer to their man.

Then murder five happened: Jayne Macdonald (25 June 1977) was walking home late one night. Her body was found by children the next day. She was only sixteen and was not on the game. The public outrage was savage. Not only had the victim pattern changed: there was now apparently an indiscriminate and opportunist approach by the killer, and his victims could be of any type, age or status.

The sixth known victim was Jean Jordan, killed on 1 October 1977. She had not returned from a night out; this murder was in Manchester, the first killing outside the Leeds-Bradford conurbation. But a vital clue was left: Jean had a £5 note tucked away in a pocket. This was a new note, and the recipients could be traced; the note had gone to one of three firms in Bradford. Sutcliffe knew the note had been left, and we know that he returned to the body to find it, but it was in a secret pocket. He even stuck glass into her body in frustration.

The seventh killing was of Yvonne Pearson. The mystery attached to this is that when her body was eventually found, two months after the murder, there was a copy of the *Daily Mirror* under one arm. The paper's date was a month after the time of death, so had Sutcliffe returned to the body? It looks that way, though he denied it.

In the wood yards next to the railway station in Huddersfield, the eighth victim was found: Helen Rytka, murdered by blows of a hammer. She was one of twins and they worked the streets in town, taking it in turns to work while one waited and looked out. But Helen took a risk and the man she had was the Ripper.

Number nine was Vera Millward, in Manchester. Her body was horribly mutilated. She had been waiting for a man she knew but he did not come so in wandering around for custom, she was fated to meet the Ripper. Her body was one of the worst ever found, with the head crushed and terrible slashing across her stomach. She was found in a car park. That seems to have been a turning point, though, because the next victims were not prostitutes – they were two students and a teenager. A woman is a woman, whatever her trade or occupation, but the media and the public moral panic accelerated their responses when number ten in Sutcliffe's list of victims turned out to be a teenager on her way home in a quiet suburb of Halifax.

Savile Park, a wide recreation ground between King Cross and the stylish area of large houses and leafy roads by the infirmary (now gone) was, with hindsight, a perfect place for Sutcliffe to strike. Young Josephine Whitaker had been visiting relatives and chose to walk home across the park. She was only a short distance from her home when he struck. This was his second teenage victim. No-one was safe now. The eleventh was Barbara Leach, a student who had merely walked home on her own after a night out with friends, just before term started. Her body was found in an alley, covered with some old carpet. The twelfth victim, Margeurite Walls, was similarly just walking home. She had been working late and decided to walk home – this was about a mile away, so she was taking a risk. It was not her lucky night at all: she was beaten to death and her body was thrown into a garden.

Finally, there was another student, Jacqueline Hill, in Leeds. Again, she was not far from safety, close to her student flat, when he struck. She had got off a bus in Headingley, and Sutcliffe, who had been buying some fried chicken at a café nearby, saw her, followed her and pounced. Her fateful night was one on which she had chosen to go to a meeting of volunteer probation workers: destiny made it her last night on earth.

What about Sutcliffe the notorious prisoner? In 2010 the papers were eager to tell the public that Sutcliffe was now cured of his schizophrenia. The subject of release and rehabilitation of lifers will always be contentious, and that announcement brought the kind of dissension that Sutcliffe's life inside has always done. Andrew Willis, a former lecturer in criminology, wrote to *The Times* to point out that 'There are about 5,600 prisoners in England and Wales who are serving indeterminate sentences for public protection, and have no idea when they might be released. Many of these cases ... are not as serious as the Sutcliffe case ... this case throws some light on a confused area of sentencing.' That is the most current issue. Another correspondent in the same week expressed probably the common feeling, that if the man was able to reflect rationally on his crimes, then he should be 'given the rest of his life to do this'.

Conversations began across the land in February 2010 when *The Sun* had a headline which said: 'Ripper's Free to be Freed from Broadmoor' and explained that 'According to a source close to Sutcliffe, the medics will support his bid to get out of Broadmoor.' The paper knew how to increase sales; the story was that no less than top security hospital doctors had told Sutcliffe's lawyers that he was now classified as a low risk prisoner. Other papers reported more soberly that there would be a medical report on him produced by the end of 2010.

The main experience Sutcliffe has had in prison, though, is that of being a victim of physical attacks. There have been six serious assaults on him, the most recent being in December 2007, when he was stabbed near his right eye while he was eating. He had lost his sight in the left eye in 1997. In this latest attack in Broadmoor, Patrick Sureda screamed at Sutcliffe and then grabbed him, saying, 'I'll teach you, you bastard, for killing all those women.' Sureda is a paranoid schizophrenic and he saw where he needed to focus the attack – on the right eye. He had a blunt seven inch blade with which he stabbed several times at his victim as he sat in a small cafeteria on the Dorchester Ward. Sureda was jailed for the murder of his mother; he was determined to use his violent skills to harm Sutcliffe, and it seems as though Sutcliffe rocked backwards automatically, probably saving his good eye from damage. Nurses then restrained Sureda and put him in isolation.

It was later reported by staff that Sureda had been 'Looking around a lot, messing with his food, but not actually eating any of it.' Then he suddenly got to his feet, and he was hold of a metal dinner knife. That is an odd detail: metal cutlery is banned in prisons, so it has to be asked why the Broadmoor prisoners have metal cutlery. In court in Reading, Sureda was found guilty of wounding with intent and assault in an attack. But he was unfit to plead.

The Ripper has naturally been a target wherever he has been housed. Back in 1983 he was in Parkhurst and with him there was James Costello, a man convicted of possessing a firearm, and who had had nine court appearances related to violence. He was waiting for a transfer to Broadmoor when he attacked Sutcliffe with a broken coffee jar.

It is well known in jails that eating times and transit times are the points in the prison regime at which attacks are most likely to be made, and this was typical of that. Costello gave Sutcliffe four wounds, including a deep slash from mouth to neck and another from the left eye to the ear. Sutcliffe had gone to a recess for water and there Costello struck. The day after the attack, his solicitor made this announcement: 'The prison doctor and the visiting professor have sectionalized Sutcliffe under the Mental Health Act. Moves will continue to get him transferred to a secure psychiatric unit.'

In court when Costello was tried, Sutcliffe was asked if he still 'heard voices' and he answered yes to that, but Costello had tried to argue that Sutcliffe's voices were telling him to kill him (Costello) and Sutcliffe denied that. In the end, after slanging matches in court between the two prisoners, the judge, Lewis McCreery, gave Costello a five-year sentence and added, 'You are one of the most dangerous and evil men it has ever been my misfortune to encounter.'

In 1996 Sutcliffe, now in Broadmoor, answered a knock on his private room door. A man called Paul Wilson was there, ostensibly to ask a favour. But he had in his hands a flex from headphones. He attacked Sutcliffe and tried to strangle him. The Ripper shouted for help and two men came to help (one being Kenneth Erskine, the Stockwell Strangler) and the Ripper was saved. Wilson said his motive was that he detested sex offenders. There was no investigation. The manager of the special hospital made no comment to the media.

The final serious attack came in 1997 from Ian Kay, jailed for attempted murder and labeled as suffering from a serious personality disorder. He attacked at a time when there were criticisms of security and care of prisoners being carried out in a review by the Health Secretary. Sutcliffe was sitting in his room when Kay attacked; a pen was used to stab the Ripper in both eyes, after objecting that he was kept so close to the notorious killer. The press were told: 'Kay has made a couple of attacks on patients in the last few months and Sutcliffe seems to have been his ultimate aim.' Earlier, Kay had planned to use one of the standard improvised weapons of prison life – a toothbrush with a razor blade inserted. But the missing razor had been traced by staff. The real reason for the attack was surely to attain the status, the 'cred' of being the man who 'did the Ripper'.

There is another side to the Ripper's prison life though: his fan mail. In his life inside he has been inundated with letters; in 2006, one report on his fan mail claimed that his brother had said, 'He has told me there are hundreds of letters stacked up. A lot of them are from women. He has had women writing to him for years. They seem to have a fascination for him because of who he is. It's amazing they would want to court a killer like Peter.' The fans continue to send letters, and in fact he is now engaged to one women, Pam Mills, who visits him, as does his wife, Sonia. This is a classic example of the irresistible allure of killers inside, as the number of women who write to US men waiting to die on Death Row testifies.

It was reported by BBC News in 2001 that Sutcliffe receives an average of thirty letters a week. A television documentary was produced, with the title, *Dear Peter – Letters to the Yorkshire Ripper* – and the programme featured people with a range of reasons for writing, including Sandra Lester who started writing to him in 1990 and gives as her reason the aim to 'extend a Christian hand of support'. He did not want her to visit, however. More interesting is Olive Curry. She has always been convinced that Sutcliffe, who visited her canteen in Sunderland when he was working as a lorry driver, was with 'Wearside Jack' – not the one who has been caught and imprisoned, but another character.

Why does Sutcliffe write so many letters? Dr George Erdos, a psychologist, explains that 'People who kill women, particularly prostitutes, do it for reasons of inadequacy ... they don't like women or they're frightened of them. Being in prison ... means there's little chance to vent that aggression. This way, he can manipulate women by telling them how special they are . . . It's a sadistic thing to do.'

Why write to crazed psychopaths? The main reason is to try to understand the mind with such a complex level of deviance and violence, but of course, these people are established subjects of professional psychiatrists, so everything there is to be known about the subject will be in print in the journals and books. Sutcliffe has said that some people have written and cultivated a relationship with him simply in order to gather material for a book about him.

The literature on Sutcliffe extends from the pot boilers that set out to exploit the notoriety and merely explain the gore and the maniacal attacks, to the serious, imaginative and thoughtful book, *Somebody's Husband, Somebody's Son* (1984) by the late Gordon Burn. Naturally, such a serial killer will continue to attract writers and publishers who want to monopolize on the commercial side of his crimes and identity, but as far as his prison life goes, the fact is that we are monitoring the pathetic decline of a maligned, physically wrecked person who is sometimes explained as 'demonic' and sometimes as a 'schizo'. Whatever line is taken on him, the result is that he has a sickness, a deviance, which is thankfully rare.

CHAPTER 18

Beverley Allitt:
Bring Me The Innocents

Planning this chapter, it was hard to avoid the feeling that the case of Allitt is totally separate from every other one in this collection. In her story there is no gang; there is no overt criminal life in the community; there was never a criminal trajectory with which she can be seen in retrospect. More exceptional than this, her crimes demand a certain degree of understanding, as she undoubtedly had severe mental problems during her murderous period while in charge of children at Grantham and Kesteven Hospital in 1991.

This story begins with the subject of Munchausen's Syndrome by proxy (MSBP). In some notable philosophical works in our time, several writers have argued that advanced capitalist culture, with massive urbanisation and consequent disintegration of a sense of an integral community, deviance has taken forms which are not overtly 'criminal' in the sense that behaviour may be invisible, submerged or unknown. One expression of this deviance from the norm is in professional guise. If a person with a flimsy sense of self works within a profession, the results may be disastrous and the crimes heinous. That was the case with Beverley Allitt. Add to the nature of some mental illness as being submerged and hard to locate, the notion that fantasy plays a major role in deviance, and there may be some understanding of why Allitt was able to murder four children and injure five more while she was working as a nurse, in a State Enrolled capacity – the SEN nurse we are all familiar with. The hard fact of how she took these young lives is that she injected them with potassium chloride or with insulin. She was working in a position of power over life and death, and all the time her own personality was severely disordered.

Fantasy, in its more potent and individualised sense, is far from harmless. The heart of the problem is a fragile ego. The term 'Munchausen' stems from a German soldier of that name who tended to exaggerate his stories of the wars, but beneath the simple feature of pretended illness there lies something more complicated. The person has low self-esteem and tends to look for strategies in life that will give them power, control and status. The person with MSBP is essentially projecting a self into a community be means of exaggerated roles and actions, so that there will be responses of respect and admiration. A vein of 'martyrdom' can run through their behaviour, as sacrifice and devotion can of course easily gather admiration.

The crimes committed under the aegis of this illness are difficult to detect, and that is where Allitt's story begins. As a child she wore wound dressings on her body so that heads would turn and sympathy would be elicited; she was overweight when young, and her lack of physical grace and appeal would only have served to exaggerate her need to be respected and noticed. Typical of the MSBP type, she frequented hospitals with imagined illnesses, and this led eventually to her perfectly healthy appendix being removed. Even that was not enough: she messed with the scar, in a way very similar to the self-harmer. Self-harm does not occur as a means of seeking attention: it is an observable symptom of inner angst and pain, with also the added dimension of self-loathing and remorse. In MSBP, this is inverted so as to be an action indicative of an appeal for notice and admiration.

With this background, the question arises: how did such a person come to be a nurse, responsible for caring for infants? People, speaking with hindsight after the offences were done, noted that in her nurse training she did some strange things, such as smearing walls with faeces. In one relationship she claimed to be pregnant when she was not actually in that condition. The track record was not exactly indicative of her having a successful nursing career, but surprisingly, she was given a temporary contract at the Grantham and Kesteven Hospital in 1991. It has to be said that there was a staff shortage: on her day shift there were just two trained nurses, and on the night shift there was only one. In effect, that meant that Allitt had plenty of opportunity to be alone with her young victims.

Liam Taylor was just seven weeks old when he was admitted to the hospital with a chest infection; he was murdered on 21 February. The other killings were to take place between then and 22 April, when little Claire Peck died after being admitted with an asthma attack. She was put on a ventilator and left in Allitt's care. There she had heart failure, was resuscitated but again had a cardiac arrest and died. Allitt was fond of injecting potassium chloride (KC1) and this causes at its least harmful gastrointestinal irritation; at its worse, on infants and patients weakened for other reasons, it causes heart failure.

Allitt's reign of 'caring' murder was later to have the media dub her 'The Angel of Death'. How could that kind and caring, dedicated young nurse be linked with the high level of deaths among the infants in her ward? That was the initial thinking. But suspicions were aroused, and police were called in. Allitt had been the only duty nurse at the times of all the deaths.

At her trial, she was charged with attempted murder and grievous bodily harm; found guilty on both charges, she was sentenced to thirteen concurrent sentences of life imprisonment. The ruling there was that she should be in custody until 2032, and even then there would have to be a certainty that she was not a danger to the public. She launched an appeal against this. Then, in 1993, there was a clamour for a public inquiry into how these deaths happened, and how and why Allitt had such power and autonomy to act in that way. At the court of appeal, this call was rejected: two staff unions were refused the right to appeal, in opposition to the ruling by the then Secretary of State for Health, Virginia Bottomley. There was already an inquiry in place, led by Sir Thomas Bingham, and the court accepted that this was sufficient. A spokesman said at the time: 'The effectiveness of this kind of inquiry depends not on the procedure adopted but on the integrity, energy, skill and fairness of the tribunal and in particular the chairman. Mrs Bottomley explained her position by saying that she wanted the same questions answered that the parents of the dead children did, and she promised a full investigation.

At the High Court in 2007, Allitt's appeal was heard. The decision was that she would serve the thirty years which was at first recommended. The life she has at Rampton High Security Hospital will continue. Mr Justice Burnton summed up: 'The impact of these offences does not require to be described and could not be exaggerated. Young lives were cut short at their inception. One of the parents commented: 'I don't think the press will ever forget, and the police who were involved in it – because it was such an horrendous story at the time, something that you never thought would happen in this country.'

The Angel of Death had emerged from a narcissistic personality – her mind shifted from the visible status her uniform gave her to the unchecked exercise of the power and opportunity Allitt craved in order to fulfil the fantasy. The word 'fantasy' in its most negative application falls short of what the nature of her killings did, to kill infants and to permanently affect other lives, profoundly and very painfully. It is never possible to explain her motives in plain terms: all that can be surmised is that the extinguishing of lives under her control was an extension of the status her position gave her. In other words, the sick mind says, 'I have this position and I am part of this profession; therefore I can take the lives I have under my jurisdiction, as well as save those lives.' At one end of the spectrum it could be argued that the action to kill was an act of mercy; but that only comes from a diseased mind who turns around the situation of normality in which healthcare does and should operate.

For Beverley Allitt, a life in Rampton will be, ironically, an existence in the milieu her mind longed for. But that life is contained by the walls and the keys.

CHAPTER 19

Charles Bronson: Prison Superstar

Charles Bronson, aka Michael Peterson, is the most publicised prisoner in the establishment of Her Majesty's prison service. In an astounding case of a prisoner's writings going into print, he leads the field. Not only have we had his autobiography, simply called *Bronson*; we have also had his guide to the prisons across the land: his *Good Prison Guide*. His public image and his cultural impact have had ambivalent responses. Some would say that he had increased the knowledge of prison life and that his books discourage younger men to follow his pattern of life, while others might reason that his writings, drawings and general image assert the glamour that so many young cons want to revel in and attain.

Freddie Foreman tells a story of Bronson in Full Sutton. Bronson had come out of his cell one morning, looking for revenge: 'Charlie jumped out into the passageway like Rambo. He was stark bullock naked, covered from head to toe in black shoe-polish and only wearing a bandanna round his head. Wielding a table leg in one hand and a broom handle sharpened into a spear in the other, he raged down the passageway. 'Foreman found him in a recess, ready to fight, and he and some friends managed to coax Bronson into having a bath to wash off the black, and talked him down. The usual army of officers was ready to charge him, and so the situation was defused. That encapsulates the nature of Bronson inside prison walls. The life inside has become his destiny and he has made it his vocation and his specialist subject, should he ever sit in the *Mastermind* chair. His book written as a guide to all the prisons he has known shows once and for all just how far he is ahead of all other prisoners in knowledge of the prison estate.

It is human nature to be interested in transgression; we there-fore also have to maintain that curiosity when it comes to the consequences of that action. From being little children, we know that the world contains checks and restraints on our urges and deeds: prison is merely an enlargement of that, with a mix of retribution and correction. It is there primarily to rehabilitate, but only 'works' in some cases and all the factors affecting the change of the prisoner are variables. With Bronson, these never worked, from the very beginning.

A summary of his prison record shows that from his first term of two months for criminal damage in Risley Remand Centre in 1969 to his present residence in Wakefield's 'special cages' he has had 160 jail stretches, and that time has included spells in several top security jails and even time in Broadmoor.

But he is a man of paradoxes and extremes. I once inter-viewed a head of education in one prison, and we talked of Bronson's time there. The manager produced a long letter, written to him by Bronson, describing just what satisfaction he derived from working with a party of handicapped people who came into the prison to use the gym every week. I worked in that gym when I wrote my documentary book, *A Good Stretch*, and I saw for myself exactly what some cons are capable of. I have an abiding image of a young man who was in and out of prison all the time, and yet who was bouncing on a trampoline, holding an older man who was in the visiting party. They were both beaming with pleasure. That would have been the kind of delight Bronson experienced and the satisfaction he took in helping these visitors to enjoy themselves.

That side of him is not acknowledged quite enough; however, this is also the man who took a lawyer hostage in Bullingdon prison in 1996, and then did the same with a doctor in Winson Green jail in 1996; his love of taking hostages led to his holding a teacher as a hostage in HMP Hull for forty-four hours in 1998. He also played a part in the Hull prison siege in January 1999.

Explaining Bronson's criminal behaviour has been problem-atic. He said on one occasion that he had been suffering from head pains and blackouts since 1975. He has described having pains on one side of his head for a long period and then black-ing out after that. He has spent an immense amount of time alone, and he has known the insides of several prison 'blocks' –

or segregation units – in his time. His earliest experience of that was horrendous, and he describes it in his autobiography: 'Pain is not the word. My bollocks were in agony, my body ached, my eye was cut, even my toes were throbbing. They stripped me off, then strapped me up in a body-belt. This is a leather belt that locks at the back and has a metal cuff on each hip, which locks your wrists.'

Stories of alleged brutality in the jails of the 1960s and 1970s are numerous in the books of memoirs, and whatever Bronson's nature, it must be mentioned that his early years in prison, with violent suppression being part of the regime, he has to have been made much worse by the treatment. Despite all this record of violence, hostage-taking and constant aggression against the world, Bronson is notorious for another reason: he and others who have helped him have produced some of the most authentic and vibrant prison writing in print. His reasons for writing are many, but he says in the first pages of his first book: 'I say to all youngsters who are thinking about becoming criminals, "Stop and think now. Don't be foolish. It's not worth it. You'll break your family's heart and destroy your own."'

In that context, the Hull prison riot of 1976 was an extreme example of what can happened when the lid blows off prison life and everything explodes. The official report into that riot attempted to explain the reasons for the horrendous rampage of violence: top of the list was this: 'Hull contained an abnormally high proportion of potentially violent prisoners and prisoners with known records of violence, indeed some who had participated in previous disturbances or in acts of disaffection in dispersal prisons.' As to the scale and cost of that riot, the report sum-marises: 'I do not think we should mince words. This was a riot of unprecedented ferocity, and a considerable amount of devastation was caused. The total cost of repair will be in the order of three quarters of a million pounds. I will therefore refer throughout this report to the events of 31 August to 3 September 1976 as a riot.'

Hull was again the focus of a siege in 1999, and he was tried at Luton Crown Court in February 2000, charged with criminal damage and assault. In that trial he took the opportunity to let the public know about how he perceived his prison life. He said that his life was hell and explained: 'I first came to prison in

1974 when I was twenty-one ... We are talking about twenty-six years being served. Twenty-two years of that I have been in solitary confinement. Isolated. On my own. No contacts. I suffer what you would call post-traumatic stress disorder.' He had opted not to have a lawyer because he said that he 'did not trust them'. Prison, he added, was like living in a sewer. His words were: 'I live in that room 23 hours of a 24-hour day. I am not living, I am just existing.' Building on this inhumane picture, he said that when the cell door opened, six officers came in to feed him, using plastic cutlery. His cell, he claimed, had a bullet-proof window which gave him a headache because of the unnatural light. He ended his description with, 'Everything is concrete, razor wire. I am living in hell. I hope you understand that.'

Only a few months after that, then resident in Woodhill prison, he was being taken to his cell in the prison's close supervision centre in the early afternoon when he lost control and went on the rampage. He took on twenty-four prison officers in a stand-off which lasted for five hours. The usual procedure then followed: ranks of officers in riot gear closed in and he was caught and restrained. Inexplicably, his violent antics in jail were released in a film clip called *Sincerely Yours*, in which Bronson is seen fighting a gang of officers, and also taking part in an illegal boxing match. The film derives from security camera footage and a leak occurred somewhere, such is Bronson's media presence. The Woodhill D Wing was known as 'Alcatraz' and was closed after a review conducted by the man who was then Chief Inspector of Prisons and who has since written a large-scale critique of the prison establishment, Sir David Ramsbottom.

Bronson has produced a body of writing that is like nothing else in the prison literature: what his life presents is a story of consciousness caught up completely inside the prison life. There is a 'jail head' in the prison system. This is a man whose entire waking moment is devoted to small victories in the ongoing battle with the establishment. Everything thrown at him, every small regulation and order, will be an appeal to conceive a battle plan. He knows every inch of the material microcosm of the prison: the kitchen, each wing, the education block, segregation, laundry, health care, gym, exercise yard and workshops. The plan and layout of the place are imprinted in his mind. His identity ceases to be the person known by relations and friends outside. When they visit they see only that one-dimensional figure who talks about the weather or what is on television. The man who returns to his pad is already scheming.

This is Bronson. Because so many men inside have developed that mindset, they see in him the absolute extreme of that profile: he had fought in every arena open to him. The trajectory of dissent in a prison career goes from adjudications to escalated offences, then to a reputation for trouble that sticks like superglue to his prison name and number. Charles Bronson has done this and more: he has taken it to the level of a finely tuned performance. His imagination has formed his projected self into a warrior. His endless press-ups become combative against his own standards. His confrontations become more extreme. The result has been, as he put it himself, 'The world left me behind more than a quarter of a century ago. I'm a lost man – what more can be said?'

His first stretch, after three lenient decisions made on him as a juvenile, was seven years for armed robbery, in 1974. He was born in Luton in 1952, and was often in fights as a young man, but his own account of that time is mostly of mindless escapades and adventures on the road and in petty theft. The seven-year term became fourteen years; he was released in 1988 but was free for only two months before he was arrested again. His prison life cost him his marriage: he was married to Irene and has a son, Michael. His family background was in Aberystwyth, where his parents ran the Conservative Club. In his teens, the family moved to Ellesmere Port in Cheshire. He has married again, to Saira Rehman, who influenced him to become a convert to Islam. Again, that did not last, and they were divorced in 2005 and he left the new religion behind him.

Only four years of his long prison life have been spent in the jail community: otherwise he has been in solitary confinement. The total time he has spent outside prison walls since 1974 is four months and nine days. After his hostage exploits, his last appeal against the life sentence was turned down in 2004. There was a parole hearing in March 2009 but the question of any parole was dismissed, as he had not changed attitudes and behaviour in prison.

In March 2009, he undoubtedly achieved the status of what is called now a 'legend'. This is because a feature film was made about him, with Tom Hardy in the title role. This was simply, *Bronson*, and the man himself told the press: 'I never dreamed I would ever have a movie made of my life. I have never glamorised crime or violence. All I ever do is expose the system for what it is.' He revels in being the legend, but still the paradox remains, as with so many of the subjects of this book: how do we explain the fact that Bronson may be kind and gentle with children and people with learning difficulties and yet be capable of extreme and thoughtless violence?

Peterson took the name Bronson after the actor, for reasons largely to do with the image he wanted for himself. What has happened is that he has become the myth he constructed himself: he has said that prison was always a war for him. Inside, that is a formula for long-time suffering. He has understood that the average con submits and toes the line, but he himself has fought every inch of the way on his long road as a notorious prisoner. It is hard to find a prison memoir with no mention of his name included. Yet, for all the adulation accorded him by younger prisoners, and in spite of the bizarre exploits and eccentricities, some of his attacks and hostage situations have been far from humorous. His assault on Phil Danielson, the teacher at Hull, is indicative of exactly why Bronson cannot be moving about in normal society. He dragged his hostage around the jail after punching him. The reason given, in Bronson's book, is that the teacher had criticised one of Bronson's cartoons: 'I'd wanted words with Phil Danielson, the teacher who had insulted one of my cartoons, since December ... Who was he to slag it off?' This highlights the fragile nature of his personality – he can act in a childlike way when irritated. He is so concerned to create his personal world of self-projection, of egoistic presence in the prison community, that he will take no negative statements.

What follows, in his book, *Bronson*, contradicts the ruling about publishing writing about the criminal's offences. What Nilsen has been banned from doing, Bronson has in print: he writes about what he did to the teacher and how he trashed the place around him.

The more the image of the man is contemplated, the more it has to be said that Bronson himself has kept the fight with the Prison Service alive. After all, causing a stir does fend off the boredom. He is most likely generating some new plan as I write this: every day is a prelude to a mind game. Prison officers have to live every day with this kind of devious strategy. Every movement in a prison is a tense moment. Movement means vulnerability; coming out of a pad is to be available for a vendetta or a hate attack, just as Sutcliffe was when he walked out and went to the recess. The old prison adage that 'happiness is a locked door' – when we look at Bronson from the officers' point of view – and yet there is a talent in the man which needs to be sustained and nurtured. It could be that his art and writings are enough to do that. But it has to be considered that there could be another master plan. We have to pray that he is not blacking up and sharpening a table leg at this moment.

He is in the Wakefield prison 'cage' at present (2010). Bronson has described this in his book, *The Good Prison Guide*: 'It is a cell with two doors, first one door, then behind that a second door, a caged door. The outside door is solid steel. The inner door is an iron gate with a steel mesh on it and a feeding hatch in the bottom. We are fed like beasts in a zoo . . . Our life is spent, twenty-three hours a day, caged up. You come out for one hour in the yard, alone. Never less than eight screws wait for the unlocking of the inner door.'

There is the dilemma society has with Charles Bronson and those like him: the treatment of them like animals is deemed necessary because they behave like animals, as Bronson demonstrated when he dragged the teacher around Hull jail with a rope tied around him. Yet Bronson is a creative mind, a loose cannon just as much as the wildest artists who have through history wrecked their lives without the residence of a prison cell.

If there is one abiding image that sums up Bronson and his impact on the nature and media image of prison today, it is his walk across the famous circle at HMP Wandsworth. Noel Razor Smith has called the place 'the hate factory' and Noel was there when Bronson did the walk. The story is that cons always had to walk around the area (the base level of the central tower in the old Panopticon jails the Victorians made); but Bronson defied the rules and walked across directly. Noel recalls: 'We hurried down to the recess and down to the end of the landing above the gate Charlie had entered through. And there he was. The front screw opened the gate that led to the centre and Charlie marched straight through . . . There were plenty of screws about, but they all deigned not to notice this prisoner . . .'

CHAPTER 20

Noel 'Razor' Smith: Best-selling Writer

He once was the 'frightener' for the armed robbers. While others were on look out, or were outside revving the engine of the getaway car, he was holding a gun to a poor, shivering bank customer. He was able to instil fear with his voice and his confidence. The potential victims quivered and begged for mercy. But the bags were stuffed with notes and he and his gang roared off to count the profits and go out on the town.

Today he is a well-known author and he is inside one of Her Majesty's prisons. When he was asked what he will do when he is free again, he says he just wants somewhere to live and somewhere to write.

This man is, in effect, someone the Prison Service should brag about, encourage, promote and show off as proof that time inside can change people for the better. Instead, he is struggling to maintain himself as a person who wants to weave words and change attitudes.

In 2008, a letter was printed in *Inside Time* on the subject of prisoners' blogs. It began with these sentences: 'The prison system has strictly forbidden me to write for publication or have any contact with the media – therefore my question for the prison service ... is this: according to Standing Orders and Prison Rules, convicted prisoners are not allowed to write for publication for payment. However, there is no mention or reference to prisoners writing blogs.' The Ministry of Justice replied that writing for the internet was covered in PSO 4411 which states that no writing must be done for profit for broadcast, publishing or television transmission.

The writer of the letter was Noel 'Razor' Smith, best-selling author of *A Few Kind Words and a Loaded Gun,* published in 2004. This man has become 'notorious' because he wants to express himself. The letter about blogs was an attempt to find another way to put words on paper, and in his case, the words are not glorifying his crimes. He has a crusade in mind, to try to change some attitudes.

Noel has said in interviews that prison transformed him. When he did his long stretch he was illiterate; he had missed school. Prison education brought out his creativity and used his powers of thought. In the former prison regime, before slopping out of cells ended in the 1990s, a creative person was unlikely to be noticed except in the accepted areas of a workshop or in a craft. But today there are several educational initiatives, many aimed at tackling the unacceptable figures on literacy in the prison population. Around the year 2000, as Will Self reminded us in an essay in *The Guardian,* 'Home Office figures stated that in any one year 130,000 people are or have been in prison and around 50% of these individuals have poor reading skills ... and 81% of all prisoners have writing skills below level 1.'

In prisons today not only are there classes in basic literacy, but there is also the Toe by Toe scheme, started by Christopher Morgan and the Shannon Trust. The spur for this came from a long correspondence between Morgan and a lifer called Tom Shannon which became the book, *The Invisible Crying Tree* (a new edition came out in 1996). The Toe by Toe idea is based on a 'buddy system' and a thick red handbook is used, so that in a 20-minute session as often as possible (every day, in theory) two people work on the book, tutor and student. Prison officers may act as the buddy if they wish. Morgan has said that at its launch in HMP Wandsworth, there was a sense of challenge, but that more than 200 prisoners have completed the course.

There is also now the residences established by the Writers in Prison Network, in which writers spend two days inside, working in all kinds of writing from drama groups to autobiographies, and from poetry to storytelling. Each year, six residencies are in place at prisons across the land, and products and results show that this work has a positive effect on the prison community.

All this has been in place for Noel. In a feature written by Erwin James in 2004, Noel explained how his writing began, and James wrote: 'His writing activities began as part of a business enterprise while he was in Albany prison on the Isle of Wight in the 1990s. An associate made greetings cards to sell to fellow prisoners. Smith, who was writing poetry, "trying to win the prison's annual Christmas poetry competition," would write the verses. " I haven't got a clue where it came from," he says, "It was just something I could do."'

The rest is history. His books are now on every True Crime shelf in the libraries and bookshops. That began with the help of Will Self. Behind the book and the new life inside, there was personal tragedy. Noel's son, Mark, took his own life after a spell in the young offender's jail at Feltham. Noel felt some responsibility for the death.

Noel is now notorious because of his transformation. His long criminal career began when he was a Teddy Boy and carried a razor; then later he became an armed robber, working in a team to rob banks and enjoy a wealthy lifestyle on the proceeds. He and the gang used to take two banks a month, and when he explains that life now he says, 'You've got to detach yourself. So you tell yourself you're a Robin Hood figure. If you sat down and told yourself the truth: I am a nasty, violent man, going out there and terrifying innocent members of the public ... You cut yourself off.'

His writing is, without doubt, something that aims to counter-act the glamorous True Crime volumes on the shelves, covers red like the blood described in their pages. The struggle to write has been tough. In his autobiography, he writes that he moved from small successes to large setbacks. Against the grain, he managed to be published in *Punch*, with help from John McVicar. But the first phase of the writing from prison was fraught with difficulties and, even today, in 2010, the obstacles are still there. When he wrote his first book, he recorded there the massive resource his life supplies for a potential writer: 'Some people may wonder at my extraordinary memory of events, some of which occurred more than a quarter of a century ago. Part of it is that prison is so boring that we have little to do except remember ...' He had the huge stock of writer's 'material' but prison regulations blocked the path.

Basically, he was aiming to write for money, and there is a prison service order against that. Writing is only a minor part of the never-ending action-response life of the prisoner and his keepers. For every strategy inside to overcome a problem, the authorities have to conceive of a measure to deal with it. The most irritating and potentially threatening examples of this is the use of mobile phones inside prison walls. They are strictly forbidden, of course, but they are always there somewhere, secreted with great ingenuity and not always located in spins. Now, every prison has a device called a 'BOSS' – a Body Orifice Security Scanner. This scans for hidden weapons and other objects hidden in any dark place in the human physiology. It looks like a very uncomfortable arm chair. Refusal to submit to such a scan means that there will be disciplinary action taken.

That is just one instance of something done to prevent prisoners getting involved in undesirable activities. After all, there are cases in which a man inside has used a mobile phone to initiate a hit killing, so this is no laughing matter. But what about the use of a pen or a keyboard in order to express what is bubbling up in the prisoner's imagination? Writing is one of the most basic human needs in our society now: to be illiterate is the surest way to oblivion. We talk of 'rehab' and fail to see that creative writing, even for small profits which may be always given to charity, gives a person an immense injection of self-esteem – a kind of drug we like to think we all have, administered naturally.

Yet the obstacles remain, and Noel Smith is in the thick of the fight to write and be encouraged. Once again, he is in a scrap. One huge problem with this whole activity is nothing to do with the system and the regulations: it is that prison writing can become great literature, as in Dostoievsky's *House of the Dead* and Chekhov's *Sakhalin Island,* or more recently than these classics, Alexander Solzhenitsyn's book, *The Gulag Archipeligo.* But that success is usually linked to political status and major events. Prison itself, as in the British establishment, is something we are forced to regard as uninteresting, static, despicable and rather embarrassing to contemplate. We have a communal sense of shame, unexpressed, because we feel that, as the statistics of people locked up tops the 85,000 mark (in March 2010), there is a dark, nagging sense of failure and that we have all played a part. The politicians and papers tell us that it is down to poor parenting, the loss of family cohesions, the collapse of Christian ethics, and so on. What is forgotten or at least overlooked is the capacity for the people inside to effect a repositioning, if at least the talented ones inside are given the chance to exercise their talents in creativity rather than in villainy.

Noel Smith illustrates yet another side to the prison identity as well, and this relates to his work and to other writing and painting, or drama, done 'inside'. This is the notion of the 'Chaps'. In prison, there are criminals who have killed or assaulted victims for a few pounds or for the satisfaction of their release of aggression. There are plenty of drug-powered cons who have done despicable things to grab the cash to fuel their addiction. Then there are the old-world career criminals who have their code of values and behaviour.

These are the Chaps. I have worked with some of them, and I can confirm that there is real substance in this. A member of this elite will consider it wrong to act against a woman, or any category of vulnerable person; they despise a 'grass' and believe in communal help and support. They create a body of firm friends. There is something of the shadowy presence of Robin Hood in their thinking, yet you cross them at your peril, because they are not dreaming of Sherwood Forest and men in tights. They can pack a firm punch and when aroused in indignation they are the enemy you dread, but their capacity for faithfulness and trust is infinite.

The young, mindless and impressionable cons inside are called *scrots* or *scrotes* by Chaps, in contempt at the usual fare of bragging, superficial thinking and shallow, questionable values. The Chap is self-contained, dignified, capable of a solid, interesting discussion on something worthwhile. Prison engenders philosophers, and a reading group of Chaps is a pleasure to conduct. They also tend to have stories to tell: compelling, bizarre, eccentric, risky, wacky, sometimes childish adventure yarns. These do not involve random acts of violence; they are concerned with right and wrong when villains deal with straight-goers.

Noel has written about how he always aligned himself with this ethos. He has written very powerfully about the reasons why there is such an allure about the renegade, tearaway con, the robber and the hit man, with the young. It is linked with their treatment inside: 'On the other side, our prime examples of straight society were the bully-boy screws and cops and snidey magistrates, who had looked down their noses and passed judgement on us.'

In fact, bearing in mind the depictions of the officers of that – the 1970s and 1980s – and the violence used to suppress behaviour which was considered unacceptable in the prison regime – it is surprising that there have been so many 'Chaps' with their old-fashioned morals and values still intact when on a long stretch.

In terms of Noel Smith's real importance today – as a writer – it has to be said that despite the massive efforts of people such as Julian Broadhead, who has published and supported prison writing, the Waterside Press, which used to publish anthologies of creative writing from prison, and of *Inside Time*, there are still many hurdles blocking the path to success for the prisoner who wants to make a career as a writer. Many people inside find their writing talents working for the in-house prison magazine, or in writing poetry for other inmates, as Noel Smith did. But when it comes to taking that step from amateur to professional, the support and permission are just not there.

CHAPTER 21

The Krays Inside

Iwant you to get a little team together and have a go at the Krays'. That was what Leonard Reed was told by his superior officer in 1964. He had been involved in the hunt for the Great Train robbers and when he started to try to work on the Kray case he was not exactly sanguine in his hopes of a breakthrough. So many people linked with their protection rackets and other schemes were afraid to talk to the law, naturally. But he selected the men who were to make up his squad and set up camp at Tintagel House. Nothing could really be kept from the Krays if it was happening in London and they knew about him. The link in the chain of potential informants broke when Leslie Payne talked to the detectives and from that moment Read had a chance of success. It was all down to the assembling of the right men, on Read's part.

That was Nipper Read's fundamental skill: he knew people and assessed character very acutely. The Krays had stepped up to murder and Jack 'The Hat' McVitie had disappeared. There were suspicions of course, but the Krays escaped from the heat for a while, holidaying in Cambridge and Suffolk. It was then that Read was busy.

Read was a short man but he was strong and athletic; like the Krays, he was a useful boxer, and he had acquired that nick-name of 'Nipper' in his early fighting days. He was only five feet seven but personality was his virtue and he had charisma. Promoted to Detective Superintendent, he set to work. He had found quick promotions in the Metropolitan Police and he was one of the youngest men to hold a senior position. But there were considerable obstacles in the Kray case. First, there was no evident collation of information about their criminal network; the men he chose were picked for specific talents. John de Rose was Head of the Murder Squad and Frank Cater was chosen as Nipper's assistant. He set a target of three months to clear up the case.

The main elements in the operation were to be to help the essential unobtrusiveness by varying routes when at work; put a stress on the security of the team members and to explore the long trail of pain and devastation they had left in the lives of their victims in past years. Read sorted through the people in that history and ended with a list of thirty – his 'delightful index' as he called it. Read expressed the beginnings of this unique challenge in his memoirs: 'This is what always appalled me when I first started the enquiry. You'd talk to the CID officers and they'd say, "Oh this is down to the Krays" and you'd say, "Well what are you doing about it?" And the answer was they were doing nothing about it.'

As those involved were gradually interviewed, Read selected the best potential witnesses from his list, men like Sidney Vaughan, but his first arrest brought no one to testify and in fact stirred some of the Kray allies in the higher echelons, men like Lord Boothby, who had denied any relationship with the brothers in the press, other than 'business' relationships. But at that first arrest, he spoke in the House of Lords, expressing indignation at the apparent detention without trial that was suspected. The trial was a mess and ended in the frustration of a set re-trial. Read would have to work hard to get it right the next time.

The Krays thought they had won and went home to celebrate, but Read gave himself six months to be prepared for round two. The break came with Leslie Payne, who knew about the murder of McVitie and thought he was most likely to be next in line. Read had him protected by installing him in a hotel in Marylebone, and let him write a long statement of his knowledge of events around the Krays' 'business'. Read saw a lot of men personally, and many faded away, not interested in helping. But Payne was a key figure and here was huge success at last. Payne fitted into the Krays' empire as the financial brain. Read explained his role: 'He was the man who had made fortunes for the twins by setting up cells of Long Firm frauds. He was far more intelligent than most of those I saw, but I had to remember he was the most experienced, even brilliant, con-man.'

Payne admitted that it was the escalation of violence in the Krays that had turned him against them. Read met Payne several times and moved easily and sensitively towards having him on the side of law. The turning point was Read's question about whether Payne knew about 'The List'. That was the kit-list Ronnie had of those destined to be 'topped'. The way the twins worked in that context made sense to both men – after all McVitie had died because he kept Kray money given to him in payment for a job – a job he did not do. Read took a 164-page statement from Payne, sitting in a police section house in Marylebone.

Read then steadily gathered other witnesses, including Freddy Gore, and he was at pains to assure each person he approached that he would not be isolated, 'on a limb' as he testified. Such actions as wire-tapping then gave Read knowledge of some of the jobs effected by the twins up in Glasgow and elsewhere. He began to understand the extent of the web of criminality he was dealing with.

When ready to swoop, Read, with characteristic caution and preparation, held a pre-arrest briefing. He had to protect witnesses at the same time as he moved in, as there were so many unknown components in the Kray empire and no total trust in anyone who had spoken to him. He had cells prepared at West End Central Police Station; he checked with his surveillance teams, and then followed them back to their council flat in Shoreditch. The usual practice of an early approach, as suspects were off-guard, did the trick. Ronnie was in bed with a young boy and Reggie was with a girl. The arrest was low-key:

> When I told Ronnie he was being arrested he said, 'Yes all right Mr Read, but I've got to have my pills, you know that.' He was referring to his supply of Stematol which kept him on an even mental keel. When Frank Cater told him he could not have them he pleaded with me and asked me to bring a letter from his psychiatrist which said he had to take two a day.

After that it was a case of tracking down the minor players. The triumph was Read's and this time he had witnesses in place, dependable and protected.

At the trial, Justice Melford Stevenson completed the process of justice: Ron went down for murdering Cornell and Reg for killing McVitie. The jury took six hours and fifty-four minutes to decide their guilt. Stevenson was the judge who sent the Krays to prison on thirty-year stretches. They were both defiant regarding Read, saying that he and other officers came to try to 'put the frighteners on them' and that they told him to 'fuck off'. Read's long and careful investigation had proved that the attitudes prevailing which accepted some powerful gangs as unassailable were defeatist and that they were in fact denying police work and taking the concept of professionalism down several pegs. He had the prise as well as the determination to take on the most powerful outfit in London and indeed beyond the city, as he gradually learned as the truth about the Kray empire was revealed.

According to some commentators, Read had also had to fight the 'mandarins on the fifth floor' at the Yard. Read was aware of some officers who had applied misguided loyalty to the wrong men. That footnote to his career only serves to increase the opinion that he was a 'reader of men' before he was anything else as a policeman. Clearly, Read was one of those detectives who had to work with total integrity in all contexts, as in the story of his being involved in a raid on a bookmakers in Albany Street when the phone rang and it was the voice of a fellow detective wanting to put a bet on. Tactfully and professionally, Read said, 'Sorry Sid, not today.'

Simply to say the word 'Krays' is to invite stock responses about them and their reputation. The public image is full of paradoxes and contradictions. The huge library of publications and films about their criminal careers offers the reader a complex assortment of puzzling suggestions about who they were and what they did. Some photos show them at ease with showbiz celebrities such as Barbara Windsor, Victor Spinetti and their pin-up gangster hero, Hollywood actor, George Raft. Others depict two bruisers, blocks of muscle who would be ideal frighteners and doormen. These images do indicate the paths their lives took, from young boxers through to long-term cons.

My main focus here is on the prisons stretches, as there is so much that is easily available on the crime elsewhere in print. For Ronnie Kray, his life ended just after a last visit to hospital.

One August Sunday in 1995, at the Heatherwood Hospital in Ascot, the medical registrar got a call from Broadmoor. The prison doctor told him that one of the prisoners had collapsed and had low blood pressure. There were no other obvious signs, but he had a long cardiac history and a Dr Blackwood was treating him for angina. The patient was Ronnie Kray.

The doctor arranged for a transfer to casualty at Heatherwood for an assessment, and Ron came in, cuffed and flanked, as the doctor told me, 'by two enormous prison guards'. The doctor at the time had no idea who the prisoner was, although the nurses did. The doctor recalled when I interviewed him, 'He cut a really pathetic, forlorn figure, yellow fingers from smoking, short, about my height ... and had a drug card as long as the Declaration of Independence which was a who's who of psycho-tropics ... [drugs affecting the central nervous system and causing changes in perception and behaviour] and he was completely and utterly compliant. He had a basic assessment (ECG, bloods and so on). His blood pressure was low ... his HB came in as just slightly low ... let's say around 11.5 with normal range for males being 12.5 to 16.5. He had a slowish pulse which I attributed maybe to the drugs he was on, but to make sure I wasn't missing anything I also did a digital rectal examination, which was normal. So about an hour later I sent him back, suggesting observation and adjustment of his medication.'

The doctor continued: 'Later I got a call from the same prison doctor saying that Ronnie had collapsed again he was really not happy to see him kept in jail under those circumstances. That's when I learned that Ronnie had had some blood tests not long before and then his HB had been quite high – perhaps around 15 or 16, which is typical of a smoker). Knowing the normal value for Ronnie meant that the blood test I had done was actually quite abnormal for him because he was missing four grams or four pints of blood. I admitted him immediately. 'Ronnie, who had been judged to be criminally insane and so sent to Broadmoor, was at that time in the same ward as Peter Sutcliffe, and he had been smoking over a hundred cigarettes a day. Doctors had told him that such a habit would kill him, and he had written a letter to Reg which made his brother become convinced that Ron had given up on their shared dreams of one day living abroad.

The doctor explained that Ronnie was most likely bleeding internally, and perhaps had an ulcer; he was then given some fluids and transferred to Wexham Park Hospital in Slough. There they had full endoscopic facilities and other specialities. During recovery, though, Ron had a heart attack and died.

Reg was in Maidstone prison when he heard of his brother's death. He heard it on the radio and was, as the first report said, 'absolutely distraught'. Reg was to die in October 2000, given his release as a dying wish. He had terminal cancer and had been given a few weeks to live. The letter Ron had written to him had these words:

Dear Reg,

I have reason to believe I will never get out.

I feel a bit sad tonight, as much as I have resigned myself to the fact that I won't be getting out. I would have loved to have come to India, China and all the other beautiful countries. But I hope you will visit all these places, as that will compensate me, if you go instead . . .

The road to those two deaths had started when they were both convicted at the Old Bailey on 5 March 1969 after a trial that lasted for forty days. Ron was found guilty of the murder of two men, Cornell and Jack McVitie, and Reg was an accessory after the fact in the case of both murders. Charles Kray, along with Frank Fraser, were accessories after the fact of the McVitie murder. The twins were given life imprisonment.

There was an appeal hearing in July 1969 on the basis of legal procedure. It was groping at straws, really, the issue being whether or not two charges of murder were proper in one indictment. The trial first held was not open to objection, either, and the reason given by the appeal judges, headed by Lord Justice Widgery, is interesting with regard to how the usual Kray methods of bullying and intimidation had failed them:

Held, further, that the joint trial was not open to objection by reason of the fact that a co-defendant (who was acquitted) in laying the foundation of a defence of duress exercised on him by the leaders of the gang, held in the course of the trial given evidence of threats and acts of violence by the leaders of the gang and their supporters, which was relevant and admissible on the issue of duress.

In other words, the Krays had no way out; a life in prison awaited them. The bullying had not worked this time. As far as Reg was concerned, the prison life was manageable, as he said himself in the book the Krays did with Fred Dineage: 'It's because of my own attitude to prison life, because of my mental approach to my problems, because of my friends, my hobbies and my fanaticism for physical fitness that I have not been sent insane.' He thought that the authorities wanted him to crack, to lose mental strength, so they could 'send me to a madhouse for ever'.

The murder of Cornell was centre stage in the court discussion. The appeal court report summed up the story: 'On the evening of March 9, 1966, the twin brothers Ronald and Reginald were drinking with a number of their associates in a public house called *The Lion*, from which Ronald Kray and the applicant Barrie drove to another public house nearby called the *Blind Beggar* where, according to the barmaid, Ronald shot Cornell in cold blood whilst the latter was drinking with others in the bar ... Ronald Kray and Barrie returned to *The Lion*, whereupon several witnesses spoke of an immediate exodus of the Kray twins ...' Forever after that, in the Kray story, the witnesses were branded 'Traitors'. The Kray story had been that, in the words of the appeal court summary, '... they had been drinking at *The Lion* and that they had later gone to the *Chequers Inn* at Walthamstow, but explained that they did this on hearing that the murder had been committed and for fear of being suspected of complicity.'

The judge was in no mood to listen to discussion about the minutiae of procedure. He said, replying to the claim that felonies and misdemeanours may be joined in the same indictment, or that a series of offences could not be lumped together, 'The court does not accept either of these arguments.' That was his plain and simple answer.

Reg's accounts of prison life cover a wide span of characters and experiences, including his time with Harry Roberts in

Gartree, when he recalled that Roberts was scared of the sight of blood. Reg wrote: 'Hate 'Em All Harry they used to call him and I believe he killed three coppers without a hint of remorse. Yet I saw him scream and nearly faint one day when he cut his finger on a knife he was using to cut up his meat ... He told me he couldn't stand the sight of blood' Reg recalled to Dineage.

When they were sentenced, they were split up: Ron went to Durham and Reg to Parkhurst. Despite a campaign to get them put together, they never were; for Reg the survival skill was mainly exercise, but he also painted. For Ron, the solace in Broadmoor was poetry. Ron told Fred Dineage that he was all right 'as long as he had his drugs'. He had to have injections of Modicate for his schizophrenia; he explained that he imagined people were plotting against him if he was without drugs. He said, 'It's a terrible feeling and it's the only time I feel out of control, like some devil has got inside my brain and is pulling it apart with his bare hands. But the drugs make everything feel fine.'

As for their creativity, it was therapeutic. Poetry in prison is almost always rhymed, with insistent rhythms, and often deals directly with the mainstream themes of remorse, coping, loved ones and dreams of freedom. For Ron, it could be, as for so many, a retrospective exercise, as when he wrote a poem about a blind friend he had when he was young, and these lines are typical: 'He could see no more, but the memory/of his friend's faces he would have in store/God was his guide; and, he knew that He/would show him the way he had never lied.'

Painting is very popular in prison workshops and classes. Every year artists compete for the prestigious Koestler Awards. When the new Home Office was set up in 2007, an artist from one jail had a watercolour hung on the walls there. To spend time in a prison art class and scan the walls of products is a wonderful experience. The works are sold for charity in many cases, and the entries for awards are always celebrated in the press and in prison publications. Reg Kray's work came from early in his life; amazingly, he was given tips and advice, when he was younger, by the great artists, Lucian Freud and Francis Bacon. The aspect of Reg's work which created most impact in the media was his charity sales in aid of the Addenbrookes Children's Liver Transplant Fund. Prisoners joined in with

Reg, and at an auction, in Cambridge, a sales auction took place, with the title of Rogue's Gallery, and the profits were very considerable.

In July 2008, eight paintings by Ronnie Kray, who also dabbled, were sold for £16,500, painted when he was in Parkhurst. His details and prison number were on the reverse of the paintings, which were in oil, and on card. Their work was often used for barter inside, and one curious story is of oil paintings which were won in a card game and sold at auction in West Chiswick, and the pictures of a river and green valley were sold for £2,000. A spokesman for the auction company told reporters, 'Reggie always painted with a dark sky. This might reflect his state of mind and the dark thoughts he had. He was known for his moods and for being aloof. Ronnie, on the other hand, always painted a white cottage because that was his idea of a dream, a place in the country.'

What about Charlie Kray? He died in HMP Parkhurst on 4 April 2000. Reg was given compassionate prison leave to join relatives at the funeral. Charlie, aged seventy-three, was in jail for running a cocaine-smuggling operation. He was serving twelve years. At the funeral, Reg was handcuffed to a female prison officer at the service, which was held in Bethnal Green, at St Matthew's Church. The BBC reported: 'Inside the church Reg moved up the aisle smiling and shaking hands with some of the 250-strong congregation, including old friends and under-world associates like "Mad" Frankie Fraser. The funeral was a much more low-key affair than that of Reggie's twin brother, Ronnie, who died in 1995. After the service, Charlie's coffin, carried by six pallbearers, was given a guard of honour by a group of Hell's Angels.'

Charlie was the first son of Charlie and Violet Kray. He joined the navy, then later retired from boxing as he was ill, and managed the careers of the twins, who were also originally destined to be boxers. He was always the brother in the shadow: the detective who arrested Ron, Nipper Read, said, 'When the twins were in trouble, Charlie was the first person they would turn to.'

The Kray story, even when they were locked up and when they died, has been one of ambiguity and mixed responses. It has to be, given that the twins were convicted of murder and that they instilled fear into so many people around them at their height of activity. But in prison, they were like all others inside: bored, in need of constant vigilance, and existing in the usual routine. Their myth will go on, as more films will be made and more books written, and maybe the truth about them will slip away.

To illustrate just how far they have permeated our iconography of the sub-culture of crime, the photographer, David Bailey, took their picture and created the classic shot of the three brothers, suited and smart, gazing in different directions, faces almost seemingly carved in stone, which appeared in his book, *Box of Pin-Ups*. He recalled, in *The Times* in March 2010: 'I didn't know Charlie very well, he was a bit of a pussy cat, but Reg and I were great friends. I used to go to his clubs with him and to the pub. He used to tell me too much about what they were up to and I used to say, "I don't want to know." And he would say, "Dave, I wish we'd done it legit like you." '

In Bailey's words, *I don't want to know,* we have the fascination and the paradox: we do want to know but also we don't want to know. After all, those men in their smart suits and well-oiled sleek hair killed, intimidated and ruled a part of London with fear. We should detest and revile them. Many people take the view that in prison the point is to 'put them in a dark hole and piss on them' as I have heard said many a time. Yet many of us want to know more. It's a matter of sheer human curiosity. There but for the grace of God go I . . .

The Kray story involves so many hooks into other areas of life. They are now just as prominent in London history as standard social historical subjects in the heritage and oral history memory. They may never have planned the notoriety, but others certainly saw them as money spinners in their image as well as in their actual crimes.

Conclusions

Notorious prisoners are destined to be in the 'shock horror' books on the shelves, and they will almost certainly exist in the public imagination somewhere between myth and a twisted celebrity glamour. The foregoing biographical profiles demonstrate, I hope, that prison lives are far from glamorous. The most tough-minded and resolute old lags become shadows of the human beings they once were. Charles Bronson wrote: 'The first thing that hits you when you're banged up with long-term prisoners is the dead eyes.'

In my own prison work, I noticed how potent the True Crime books in the library were: they were popular and people could never have enough of works about the Krays, gangland and auto-biographies of known villains. I once started a reading group in one jail, and I wanted it to be like any other reading group – works selected across the range of fiction, biography and maybe other genres. I asked men to suggest titles, and after a few conversations the general feeling was that we should have a reading group devoted entirely to True Crime. I thought that such a group was better than no group at all, and I selected the first two books. We started with a memoir by one of the Great Train Robbers. It was in small print and it included a great deal of detailed biography.

At the first meeting of the group, it was clear that nobody had read it. One man said, 'I read the first three pages, then dropped off to sleep.' That was the feeling of all members, so I moved on to the Tony Martin case and a book written about that. It was a huge success, because it raised an issue that mattered to them. Some of them did burglaries and robberies of course, and they felt that the law should protect them when they went onto another person's property to steal. Being shot in the back as

Martin's victim was, did not seem right at all. Our debate lasted for an hour.

That experience sums up the nature of prison thinking and criminals' interests. Prison is circumscribed thinking: it creates obsession and mindsets that run around on a loop. Press a button and rant number one begins; press another and rant number two follows. But I also have to say that in any random group of people inside, there are some really original and fascinating imaginations at work, and a jail is a buzz of creativity. The insides of prison walls teem with stories. Compelling stores are generated every day. As I arrived at each prison car park, I felt that thrill of the unexpected every time. Anything could happen in a prison day, and a 'normal' one was hard to find.

'Notorious' prisoners exist in a world fabricated by the media. Inside the walls, the staff have to cope with them; every day brings moans, complaints, petty irritations. One little event at home can disrupt the day. In my drama groups and writing groups, I could always tell when someone had received some bad news. It could be a phone call from a mother or a wife, about debt, or illness or the kids at school. At its worse, the change of mood could be after a court hearing and a 'knock back' in the sentencing. Sometimes it was a falling out with a wife or girlfriend. I always had to guess, and then ask questions if necessary later.

Even the most high-profile prisoners share those same concerns. The career criminals who have never done anything truly nasty and violent rub shoulders with the ones who have a transient glamour, the ones whose names might be in the papers. That encounter has to be made normal. In a jail, everything must be contained for the common good – and that includes the brimming anger and rage of the individual who is frustrated and takes it out on the nearest person to him.

As my chapters have shown, even the prisoners whose names have reached the level of iconic status – Brady, Sutcliffe, Bronson, Krays – have to live lives in prison on a par with the mundane and routine we all have to cope with. They have to eat, sleep, defecate, indulge in small talk, play chess and attend classes or workshops. In that context, 'notorious' seems to lose its impact.

In many ways, the literature of prison life has been either written by major figures such as Nelson Mandela or Antonio Gramsci, or it has been in the genre of the shocking memoir. What has been marginal is the documentary. Although television is now making up for this omission in series broadcast on the Crime and Investigation Channel in particular, there is still very little known by the general public about the experience of prison. The people in my chapters illustrate both ends of the spectrum: the sensational and the mundane. One conclusion has to be that publishers rarely see the documentary narrative as being commercial. They lust for celebrity.

I know this from personal experience. At one time I was working with a prisoner on his autobiography. The story was a compelling tale of childhood deprivation, followed by many years inside and sentences for attempted murder. The man had taken it on himself to play the role of avenger and attack supposed paedophiles, to do what the law had not done: rub them out. I knew that this could not be published while he was doing time, but I approached a publisher simply to test out the ground as to what interest would be aroused.

The publisher was interested and I met them in London. I explained that this book was something the man would like to publish when he was released, and that he would need an editor to work with him. I explained that the Writers in Prison Network, with whom I was working, have a mentoring scheme for people such as this man. This was all very interesting, the publisher said, but wasn't Jeffrey Archer once in that prison? If so, did I have any stories about him? I was told that if I did, they would 'publish it tomorrow'.

That says everything about the dilemma of the public being informed about the real experience of jail. Some years ago, the government experimented with schemes to bring young offenders (or potential offenders) into prisons to be frightened. Prisoners would volunteer to act out typical scenes from prison life and the kids would be suitably terrified. I spoke to one man who had taken part in this. He talked about how much he enjoyed the acting and that he felt a great sense of satisfaction in having done something to try to stop young kids getting into trouble with the law. Even Charles Bronson has expressed similar thoughts.

What are we not doing then, to increase awareness? We are believing the stereotypes and seeing such programmes as *Bad Girls* and *Prison Break* because there is an attraction in prison tales – but only in those tales that perpetuate the stereotypes.

Criminologists as well as politicians would probably agree that to spend time giving attention to prison deeds and misdeeds is not advisable. I can appreciate the argument that to ignore the negative in life is to stop it from being seen and exaggerated. There is no doubt that young cons are impressionable and will soon perceive their lives to be 'us against the system' but massive amounts of money and all kinds of professionalism are aimed at rehabilitation, in the belief that such an outcome is possible. The key question, teasing every politician who might have a new manifesto and a master plan, is 'Does prison work?'

It only works for those who change radically and open up themselves to change. When I first worked in a prison, several professionals in the service said that there was a pattern: that in the mid thirties lots of villains changed and lost the fascination of the buzz that risky crime gives you. These people open up to new things; they are often where the highs of prison life is found – they try new things and their resolve to change leads them to look for outlets in which their skills and experience may find expression. This is too optimistic a picture of course, because there are also many who reach that stage and atrophy. They merely become slobs and close up, shut off any hint of change. But when you meet a man or woman who has become receptive to that transmutation in which they find a new self, the feeling is immensely satisfying.

However, there are some stories from inside which remind us of the sheer boredom, depression and limbo that come with prison. A person inside has to find ways to cope and exist or they run into trouble from all quarters – mostly from inside themselves.

On one occasion I worked with a young man who was self-harming. He had so many cuts on both arms that he looked as though there had been a massive tattooing job on him that had gone wrong. He told me that from his pad window he could see his own house, just beyond the prison walls. 'It was where my little baby died,' he said. That is one of thousands of human stories generated behind the stereotypes of 'typical prisoners'. I hope this book has helped to dispel some myths.

In spite of all these thoughts concerning the reality of prison, the media still want us to take an interest in those who are notorious in the sense that there are highly dangerous or evil convicts amongst us and that their lives and exploits will always be of interest. That story will run as long as there are tabloid papers who insist on applying the term 'evil' to prisoners, grouping all the people inside together as if evil goes with every offence. In an anonymous True Crime classic, *A Complete History of the Lives and Robberies of the most Notorious Highwaymen*, published in 1719, we have these words: 'Newgate is a dismal place ... a place of calamity, a habitation of misery, a confused chaos, a bottomless pit of violence, a Tower of Babel where all are speakers and none hearers.' Yet, in spite of that description, the villains and unfortunates of the following century were mostly placed in the stories in the best-selling *Newgate Calendar*, the classic collection of crime stories published mainly in the 1820s. The eighteenth century and Regency period were the times in which the gaolers at Newgate (called ordinaries) earned good money taking down the criminal biographies of those about to die on the scaffold.

Civilised society still wants its sordid and dramatic tales of law-breakers; 'notorious' criminals will always have stories to tell that will compel attention. In spite of all the serious reflections I have made, the fact is that there is excitement and some kind of anticipatory buzz in prison stories. Before I enter a prison, ready to work on some writing project or listen to a life story, I have that little flutter of apprehension. The professionals tell you that you are safer inside the jail walls than out walking the streets doing the shopping. That is true, but still, when we are put in a confined space several hundred people who know that others have the keys and that they cannot leave to buy a paper or have a drink at the pub, we should expect the frustrations to boil over from time to time. Riots and mutinies are rare but when they happen they are terrifying for all concerned. In a prison riot, the mainstream cons go looking for the sex offenders, the 'nonces' as they are called. There is a potential for murder there. Every day the men inside for violent crime, white collar crime or various drug offences, have to watch the 'nonces' being moved, to a workshop or to the exercise yard. In each move-ment there is a tenseness. When prisoners queue for food at the canteen hatch, there is potential violence. The trays are weapons and the opportunity, outside the protection of the pad, for attack, is too hard to resist for those bearing grudges.

Some prisoners cope very well with jail and they need the time inside. Once in a prison library book I found these words scrawled inside: *'Browny, C Wing. Doing three and luvvin' it.'* Others dread each sunrise and wake to find that the dreams of home are just dreams, and they are actually still in their pad, with the smells and the often unwelcome company of the pad mate and his bad habits and noise.

Being notorious is very difficult; being just another con is easy. So we have the literature of prison and the tales of bold and dangerous crime. As John McVicar memorably said, 'Being a thief is a terrific life, but the trouble is, they put you in the nick for it.'

An Afterword

This is a short essay attempting to make the link between the notorious and the more routine, perfunctory prison lives. There is a link, and it is about the distortions of prison life in the public mind, and also about the inescapable fact that the readership for notorious crime stories will always be there.

Many of the men in the stories in this book have been creative while doing time. Time inside for many is time 'turned in' – with no escape from the self you have to carry around. Creative writing is a valuable part of this introspection, but as the cases of Nilsen, Sutcliffe, Smith and Bronson have shown, the activity is riddled with difficulties and legal issues. Many prisoners can't wait for the next edition of the paper, *Inside Time,* to turn up in the library. It has grown over the last few years into a substantial collection of letters from prisoners, legal information and, most recently, a poetry supplement.

In my time as a writer in residence in various prisons, I worked with hundreds of offenders who wanted to see their name in print or on a stage, but their aim was not necessarily to become rich. Yes, if the writing revels in the narrative of their offence and includes an account of their victim, then the very idea is morally unsound. Yet when I was asked if I would help a prisoner write their autobiography, the glint in their eye when I agreed was rarely to do with cash machines: more often I found that it was a cathartic wish.

Of course, the glamour of true crime biographies is always there, but I would argue that the dreams of being the next Charles Bronson is limited to the young and feckless.

More seasoned offenders generally feel drawn to the profound need to communicate, to make the world aware of what their trajectory has been from crime to prison, with the mess of shattered relationships that litter their path. One of my clients had written several plays which had been staged or broadcast and all profits had been given to charity. As a writer in prison, working for the Writers in Prison Network, I was always aware that prisoners must not write for cash while under the domain of the Governor and the prison service. Yet the paradox of a case such as Razor Smith and his life as a best-seller writer worries anyone working in the arts inside prison walls. Recently, he told *Inside Times* that he was being investigated with the profit motive in mind, yet he had been encouraged to write while in his cell. After all, the isolation of life in a pad is ideal for creative writing; we have to ask what happens after the entice-ment to write creatively, to express oneself, to examine a life of drama and extreme emotion?

The answer must be that for many inside, as for those writers outside the prison walls, the writing becomes enjoyable, fulfill-ing and indeed may potentially become a source of income. If we talk of rehabilitation, then what is wrong with that? Some of my clients inside have had excellent writing published, and made no money at all, but on the other hand, an anthology I edited of women's writing from HMP Morton Hall, *The Emotional Ride*, has just won the Platinum Award in the Koestler Foundation Awards. The four writers will receive £25 each. None of the material in that book is about their victims or indeed about their crimes, in any explicit way.

Encouraging offenders to write will initially be a boost to their self-esteem, but for some it will be a revelation: they may have missed school and books may never have come their way, then suddenly they are assured that they have ability with words and they may see a future involving such activity. By all means let's suppress the kind of unhealthy wallowing in crimes that a minority of prisoners wish to do, but we should also encourage and liberate that creativity nurtured by the love of language that people such as Razor Smith wish to do. He has openly said that his books are to warn incipient gangsters of the folly and danger involved in handling guns and relishing violence.

Society generally is rarely asked to take note of anything good going on behind the high walls of the prisons in our cities. The local jails are sometimes in the midst of a town or city and at times they are in empty, barren places. In Wakefield, which is a high security prison, there has been a prison in the ironically named Love Lane since the sixteenth century, when it was a House of Correction. The jails we have are tucked away, out of sight. What we know of prisoners extends only to what the papers tell us. Television gives us tales of monsters behind bars; producers think we want to know only about the comfort zone of having killers and rapists locked up for ever. Most of us have driven at speed on a motorway and passed a 'meat wagon' – the prison van, the Group 4 as it used to be. Inside are people on their way either to court or prison. They are mostly pathetic, sad, lost characters who do not need muzzles, chains and cuffs.

Still, the prison house holds fascination. People live there and survive, and what they survive is explained by Oscar Wilde:

> All that we know who lie in gaol
> Is that the wall is strong;
> And that each day is like a year,
> A year whose days are long.

The prison service acts as a kind of patron in encouraging prisoners to write ('it stops them kicking off') but then has to apply all kinds of repression when that writing begins to succeed. As Dr Johnson said when writing to his patron, Lord Chesterfield, 'Is not a patron my Lord, one who looks with unconcern on a man struggling for life in the water, and when he has reached ground, encumbers him with help?' What is needed to make the prison authorities see themselves as patrons is a mystery. Prison memoirs again and again return to the question of why people revisit, imaginatively or as historians, their crimes, so there has to be a way to use that desire – with the exception of the most heinous and horrendous offences of course. In most cases we are talking about the mainstream category of crimes committed either as part of a concept of crime as a business or as a series of unfortunate errors and bad influences which tend to be understood only later in life when mistakes are seen for what they were in the past.

Most of the prisoners here have wanted to find some way of expressing themselves – something very different from a gun barrel or a knife. There is a link between crime and creativity, and that was spotted and written about in the Regency period in the first literary work in English which dealt with true crime as we think of it now – Thomas de Quincey's long essay, *Murder Considered as One of the Fine Arts*. De Quincey writes about murder, with the terrible Ratcliff Highway murders of 1811 in mind – as if it were one of the visual arts and he were a professor or an art historian. He had realised, a century before the True Crime in the popular press ever mentioned prisoners' creativity, that in some proportion, a prison population had talent there somewhere.

On balance, my chapters have covered a fair proportion of mindless killers and in contrast, criminals for whom jail has become almost a vocation. Indeed, for Charles Bronson, it almost seems like his kingdom and he resents others wanting any power there.

Acknowledgements

Thanks go to my editor, Brian Elliott, and to the artist, Vicki Schofield, who produced the line drawings. I also must thank A.M. and G.B. – anonymous but very helpful. In terms of the oral history I gathered in order to write these tales, several people interested in prison history answered questions and told tales.

As usual, there has been some digging in obscure works and forgotten ephemera for this project. Thanks go to Clifford and Marie Elmer for this assistance.

I also have to mention Pauline Tait, June Hanrahan, Jimmy, Mr T and my group who told tales of slopping out and worse. Also Ian Lawman has to be thanked for some new perspectives.

There is also a massive body of prison writing in ephemera and in local publications, and thanks are due to various scholarly researchers who have answered questions.

Bibliography and Sources

Books

Bilton, Michael *Wicked Beyond Belief* (Harper Collins, 2003)

Bronson, Charles *Bronson* (Blake, 2004)

Bronson, Charles *The Good Prison Guide* (Blake, 2007)

Byrne, Gerald *Borstal Boy: The Uncensored Story of Neville Heath* (John Hill Productons, 1955)

Clarke, John and Shea, Andy *Touched by the Devil* (Simon and Schuster, 2001)

Cross, Roger *The Yorkshire Ripper* (Harper Collins, 1999)

Denning, Lord *Landmarks in the Law* (Butterworths, 1984)

Dernley, Syd, with Newman, David *The Hangman's Tale: Memoirs of a Public Executioner* (Robert Hale, 1999)

Dineage, Fred *Reg and Ron Kray: our Story* (Sidgwick and Jackson, 1988)

Douglas, Robert *At Her Majesty's Pleasure* (Hodder, 2007)

Eddleston, John J *The Encyclopaedia of Executions* (Blake, 2000)

Fielding, Steve *Pierrepoint: A Family of Executioners* (Blake, 2006)

Fletcher, Connie *Real Crime Scene Investigations* (Summersdale, 2006)

Foreman, Freddie *Brown Bread Fred* (John Blake, 2007)

Fraser, Frankie *Mad Frank's Britain* (Virgin, 2002)

Gaute, JHH and Odel, Robin *The Murderers' Who's Who* (Pan Books, 1980)

Godfrey, Barry and Lawrence, Paul *Crime and Justice 1750–1950* (Willan Publishing, 2005)

Hale, Leslie *Hanged in Error* (Penguin, 1961)

Hancock, Robert *Ruth Ellis: the last woman to be hanged* (Orion, 2000)

Harrison, Richard *Foul Deeds will Rise* (John Long, 1958)

Hastings, Sir Patrick *Cases in Court* (Pan, 1953)

Hopwood, Clive *Free With Words: writers in prison* (Bar None Books, 1999)

Humphreys, Sir Travers *A Book of Trials: personal recollections of an eminent judge of the high court* (Pan, 1955)

Hyde, H Montgomery *Famous Trials: 9 Roger Casement* (Penguin, 1960)

Irving, Ronald, *The Law is an Ass* (Duckworth, 2000)

James, Erwin *A Life Inside: A Prisoner's Notebook* (Atlantic Books, 2003)

James, Trevor *About Dartmoor Prison* (Hedgerow print, 2007)

James, Trevor *There's One Away: Escapes from Dartmoor Prison* (HedgerowPrint, 1999)

Jones, Richard Glyn *True Crime through History* (Constable and Robinson, 2004)

Koestler, Arthur and Rolph, CH *Hanged by the Neck* (Penguin, 1961)

Kray, Kate *Killers* (John Blake, 2003)

Lavelle, Patrick *Shadow of the Ripper* (John Blake, 2003)

McVicar, John *McVicar by Himself* (Artnik, 2007)

Morton, James *East End Gangland* (Times Warner, 2001)

Moss, Alan and Skinner, Keith *The Scotland Yard Files* (The National Archives, 2006)

Parker, Norman *Parkhurst Tales* (Blake, 1995)

Pierrepoint, Albert *Executioner: Pierrepoint* (Coronet, 1971)

Priestley, Philip *Victorian Prison Lives* (Pimlico, 1999)

Read, Leonard with Morton, James *Nipper Read: The Man who Nicked the Krays* (Times Warner, 1991)

Rowland, John *Unfit to Plead?* (Pan, 1965)

Seddon, Peter *The Law's Strangest Cases* (Robson Books, 2005)

Smith, Noel 'Razor' *A Few Kind Words and a Loaded Gun* (Penguin, 2005)

Staff, Duncan *The Lost Boy* (Transworld, 2007)

Stokes, Anthony *Pit of Shame: The Real Ballad of Reading Gaol* (Waterside Press, 2007)

Stout, Martha *The Sociopath Next Door* (Broadway Books, 2005)

Thomas, Donald *Villains' Paradise* (John Murray, 2005)

Tibballs, Geoff *The Murder Guide to Great Britain* (Boxtree, 1994)

Wilde, Oscar *Complete Works* (Collins, 1948)

Wilde, Oscar *The Ballad of Reading Gaol* (Two Rivers Press, 2004)

Woodley, Mick *Osborn's Concise Law Dictionary* (Thomson, 2007)

Wynn, Douglas *On Trial for Murder* (Pan, 1996)

Articles

'Broadmoor Hospital Gives up its Secrets' *Converse* August, 2009 pp. 24-25

James, Erwin 'I'm on a Journey' *The Guardian* 26 May, 2004 (interview with Noel Razor Smith)

Presser, Lois 'The Narratives of Offenders' *Theoretical Criminology* Vol. 13 no. 2 May, 2009

Self, Will 'When will we Ever learn?' *The Guardian* 7 June 2005

Web Sites

www.bbc.uk/l/hi/uk

www.bullyonline.org/workbully/munchaus.htm

www.eastlondonhistory.com

www.enotes.com/forensic-science/macdonell-herbert-leon

www.express.co.uk

www.guardian.co.uk

www.prisons.org.uk

www.prisonservice.gov.uk

CD

Williams, Paul RL *The Ultimate Price: the unlawful killing of English police officers* (in two parts); also at www.murderfiles.com

Contemporary records

Court of Criminal Appeal records (Sweet and Maxwell, 1969)

Crown Cases Reserved

Old Bailey Session Papers

Newspapers and Magazines

Annual Register

Context

Daily Mail

Daily Mirror

Inside Time
Lincolnshire Archives
Sunderland Echo
The Police Journal
The Times Digital Archive
Yorkshire Post

Index